An Undertaker's Diary

Putting you in the same room as Death!

Paul R Seymour

Bloomington, IN   Milton Keynes, UK

AuthorHouse™
1663 Liberty Drive, Suite 200
Bloomington, IN 47403
www.authorhouse.com
Phone: 1-800-839-8640

AuthorHouse™ UK Ltd.
500 Avebury Boulevard
Central Milton Keynes, MK9 2BE
www.authorhouse.co.uk
Phone: 08001974150

© 2006 Paul R Seymour. All rights reserved.

No part of this book may be reproduced, stored in a retrieval system, or transmitted by any means without the written permission of the author.

First published by AuthorHouse 11/28/2006

ISBN: 978-1-4259-7608-8 (sc)

Printed in the United States of America
Bloomington, Indiana

This book is printed on acid-free paper.

Table of Contents

Preface	ix
Introduction	xi
Glossary of Terms	xiii
PLANE SICKENING	1
ON THE FIDDLE	9
M**A**NS BEST FRIEND	21
WENT TO PIECES	29
MAGGOTS!	35
THE RO**U**TE OF ALL EVIL!	41
MADE ME JUMP	49
AL**L** SALTED	55
THE AXE-MAN COMETH	59
ICE-C**R**EAM AT NIGHT!	65
TRAIN **S**POTTING	75
GON**E** SWIMMING	81
IT'S IN THE BAG	85
THANK **Y**OU FOR NOT SMOKING	89
RTA (ROAD TRAFFIC ACCIDENT)	97
ON YOUR BIKE!	103
SPLITTING **IM**AGE	109
FOR BETTER OR FOR W**O**RSE	117
FRED	125
THE REAL TERROR	135
THROUGH **U**NDERTAKERS EYES	137
Current & Forthcoming Publications	143
Website	147
20 YEA**R**S ON…	149

Please note: Although all the following accounts are based on true happenings, names, places and images have been 'altered/blurred' to protect anonymity and out of respect for the victims and their family/friends. This publication is intended for entertainment value only and it is sincerely hoped that no offence is taken from reading it.

Oh Yes and… if you are of a nervous disposition and/or are easily offended/shocked you may wish to close this book **now!**

Paul Seymour – circa 1976

PREFACE

Unless you are either very young or very *lucky* I think it's a safe bet to assume that most people reading this book have, at sometime in their precious life, encountered a funeral and/or death in some 'variety' (obviously not *their own* (unless that utter b*llshit they come out with every week on Most Spooky (or whatever on earth it's called!) is actually true of course!).

However, I think also it's a reasonable assumption that a good percentage of the (2 or 3) people likely to be reading this book are also unlikely to have encountered death on a *daily* basis for years on end (now that would make you REALLY unlucky wouldn't it!).

Of course, most people have an 'inkling' of what death is *about* (after all, it *IS* the most common thing on earth along with birth, taxes and England losing the World Cup (again!) but have you *really* stopped to wonder just how diverse a matter it really is? Just like a MacDonald's Cheeseburger, no death is alike and it always amazed me how doing the same old thing could be so 'different' day on in and how little people appreciated what 'the funeral trade' was all about (most people I spoke to seemed to think that no-one ever died on a weekend and that dying people all duly 'reported' to the funeral parlour with no intervention or help whatsoever!).

In over seven years of 'undertaking' I can honesty say that I really didn't know what was around the 'next corner' (probably another one!) and so I started to keep diaries of some of the more 'peculiar' days in my 'life of death' and it is with some (warped) pleasure that I hereby share some of these 'unique' stories with you today.

You may laugh; you may cry; and, quite possibly, you may *throw-up* (you have been warned!) but you will also get a 'glimpse' of what it is like to have to 'deal with death' for a living (irony was always one of my best qualities!).

In short, if you've ever wanted to *see though an undertakers eyes*, here's your chance so…Buckle-up (believe me, it CAN help!) and come along with me for a journey to hell and back (and don't forget the sick bag too!).

Oh yes; *one final thing…* I have tried to keep these stories 'as true to their *original written form*' as possible so, **please remember;** if you think that they look like they were written by an *illiterate 16 year old…* **THEY WERE!**

INTRODUCTION

Well, you've read THIS far so I'm assume that you are still 'curious' and so I thought that one last quick warning, sorry, *introduction* was in order to ensure that you know what you are letting yourself in for…

As you would; I'm sure; expect of a publication with such a title, the following pages contain some fairly graphic and gruesome descriptions (and even the odd 'gory picture' or two (though, for the sake of 'decorum' (and your sanity!), I have *'blurred'* them so that the reader can still get a 'taste' of what they are all about without taking the whole thing to *'extremes'* (my intention in writing this book was to entertain and educate not scare and nauseate the reader!) so please bear this in mind before continuing.

The following 'stories' therefore are 'not for the faint hearted' and if you continue to read on, you do so at your own risk and preference. This is your **FINAL** warning!

OK, still with us then? *Right…* The following chapters/stories are based on **REAL** events and situations that I encountered (and subsequently wrote about in the diaries I kept at the time (1975 to 1982)).

They are told pretty much in my *own words/style* and I have tried not to add, change or embellish them as much as possible (although I **have** made some minor changes to names and locations in order to protect the anonymity of some of the characters portrayed within (both living or dead!) as I feel this is only reasonable and correct (again, I wish to inform **not** offend).

Other than that, the stories are pretty much 'as I originally wrote them way back in the 70/80's (including poor grammar, lousy punctuation and 'iffy accents' (Yep, we/they really **DID** talk like that!).

I hope that you enjoy reading the stories and that you don't have too many nightmares afterwards (but, if you do, try to look/concentrate on the 'funnier sides' of them as I did and you may find that humour makes the whole thing so much *easier to bear* (I honestly believe that, had I not 'developed' (mainly as a 'defence mechanism') the warped and frankly sick sense of humour that I now find myself stuck with, I would probably have gone completely insane (as opposed to only 'mildly nutty'!) years ago!

ENJOY!

Glossary of Terms

As in many 'professions' the 'undertaking business' has its own *jargon* and so, as the following stories are 'authentic' accounts they will inevitably contain some words that will not be familiar or have no meaning to 'outsiders'.

I have, therefore, created this short glossary of *Undertaking Terms* (don't worry, we didn't use THAT many!) to both help familiarise you with the terminology used and to make the 'experiences' as 'realistic' and original as possible.

NOTE: Only the <u>UNDERLINED</u> terms are actually 'used' in the main text (I have included the rest for those curious to know more about the funeral trade).

<u>SHELL</u> – A 'temporary coffin' used for the collection of bodies from hospitals, homes, etc., Usually, several (3-6) shells were loaded on to the 'pick-up' van (see 'meat wagon') at a time which were then 'loaded and unloaded' throughout the day. Towards the latter part of my time 'at the Co-op' shells were gradually being **replaced** by stretchers which were both easier to 'manhandle' and lighter/smaller.

<u>BIG BERTHA</u> – Our 'affectionate' name for the 'double-sized' Shell (see above) which was reserved our more 'portly' clientele!

<u>MEAT WAGON</u> – Slang term for the 'Pick-up Vehicles (in our case Black Transit vans) used for the collection of dead bodies from Hospitals, Homes, etc., Note: These vehicles were fitted with large 'extractor fans' in the rear *'passenger'* compartments (for *obvious* reasons!)

STRIKE/STRIKING – The term used to refer to the action of lifting a coffin/shell into an 'upright position' when entering a lift, manoeuvring in a 'tight space', negotiating around bends, etc., Normally, the 'foot' of the coffin/shell is rested on the floor (and preferably against a 'fixed' object (even an undertakers foot would do at a pinch!) to ensure that it doesn't slip. However…only a very FOOLISH undertaker would strike a coffin/shell without **first** securing a **striking belt/rope** (see below) around it *first!*

STRIKING BELT/ROPE – A rope or long leather belt used to 'secure' the coffin lid to the coffin thus preventing the lid from falling off or from being 'forced' off by the weight of the *'contents'* during striking (see above). Without a striking rope/belt attached, the undertaker(s) run a significant risk of unceremoniously dumping the contents of the coffin onto the ground/street (a practice that, thankfully, didn't happen very often (though I must confess to having managed it once (or twice!).

PAGING – The traditional term for the 'short walk' carried out by the manager/bearer(s) in front/at the side of the hearse. It is/was normal practice for the manager and/or bearer(s) to 'escort' the funeral procession at a slow walking pace for a few hundred yards. Paging was traditionally carried out when the funeral procession left the house and, on occasions, when entering the cemetery/crematorium.

Note: Some Managers/Hearse Drivers took 'great pleasure' in trying to catch the heels of an unsuspecting bearer or 'push them along' a little (often at a rate not befitting the circumstances) or, if really lucky, forcing them into trees, puddles and alike (yes, very childish indeed!).

OUT OF ENGLAND ORDER (OEO) – Form required by Customs and Excise to permit the 'export' of a dead body from the UK

SHILLINGS – An agreed (at least at the Co-op!) payment made to staff who were 'out on the road' (whether carrying out a funeral or collecting bodies, etc.,). Payment was usually made (weekly) to those staff who were unable to make use of the subsidised canteen facilities available.

Originally the payment was 2 shillings (10p) a week but increased to nearly £3 by the time I finally left (1983).

BOX MONEY – Generic term for the tips/gratuities received by undertakers (normally the 'manager') normally at the end of a funeral. **ALL** tips were *'supposed'* to be pooled and then divided and shared equally between **EVERYONE** (coffin makers, office staff, workshop staff, etc.,).

Box money was normally paid monthly and, in our case, amounted to around £10-£20 per month (not bad for the 70's!).

Unfortunately, box money was gradually 'faded out' after much *abuse* by the managers of the funerals/offices (hence the term you never see a **poor** undertaker!).

<u>**BURNER**</u> – Slang term for someone burnt to death or, occasional, used to describe a cremation.

JOHN/JANE DOE – 'Generic' term given to a corpse that had yet to be *named* (i.e. because it was too badly injured/decomposed or because the body had yet to be identified).

DOA – Term used by Ambulance crew, etc., to describe someone that was alive (or who had yet to be certified dead) when they were 'picked-up' but who had then subsequently died/been certified dead later; Stands for Dead On Arrival.

ASHES – The cremated remains of the deceased. It is a general misconception that 'the ashes' are the 'burnt remains' of the whole body. However… in reality, the skin and internal organs were 'completely consumed' by the intense heat/flames of the cremation oven thus leaving a mostly intact *skeleton* (which was then 'pulverised' and placed into an urn/container).

NOTE: One of the most 'common questions' that I was asked when I was an undertaker was; "are they REALLY XXXX's ashes?" Well, you may be pleased to know that the answer is *YES* as the coffin/body is placed in to an 'individual' oven (marked with the name and details of the deceased) and is therefore recovered (for the most part) *whole*.

CREMATION COFFIN – The **SECOND** most burning question (sorry, no pun intended) I was asked was; "do they **REALLY** burn the coffin?"
Again, the answer is **YES...** Cremation coffins are generally made of combustible materials (chipboards, sawdust (for padding), etc.,) and are therefore DESIGNED to be burnt. That said, on occasions, some 'bits' MAY have had to be 'removed' (i.e. if someone requests 'real' (e.g. brass) handles (normally they are made of plastic) they would be removed **before** the cremation as the ovens are not designed to deal with such items (a point I discovered to some cost when I tried to hide a few brass coffin-plates that I had inadvertently damaged in a cremation coffin not realising the problems it would cause (basically, the 'pulverising machine' (see Ashes (above)) got 'clogged up' with molten metal and they were none to happy!).

FLOATER – Term used to describe someone who died by drowning or who had been 'collected' from the sea, pool, lake, etc.,

JUMPER – Term used to describe someone who had died by jumping from a tall building, etc.,

RTA – **R**oad **T**raffic **A**ccident (In 'our case' this normally referred to a **fatal** accident involving one or more vehicles).

BODY LABEL (see front cover for example) – A small (3-4 inches long) label that contained the basic details (age, sex, address, etc.,) of the deceased which was normally tied to the big-toe (or wrist, etc.,) of the body to identify it. The ones we/the Co-op used had a small 'tear-off' portion at the bottom which was removed and attached to the coffin-handle or lid to confirm identity prior to the funeral (after all; it wouldn't do to cremate the wrong body now would it!).

JOB-SHEET(S) – Daily list containing either **A.** *Funeral* Job Sheets; Instructions for all funerals in any one day (each chauffeur/bearer would collect the 'job sheet' the day before to ascertain their required duties for the following day (funeral job sheets were normally posted the day before the funerals) and also to allow chauffeurs to 'plan their routes', etc.,) or **B.** *Collection* Job Sheets; These were printed for the 'van crews' instructing them on the collection of bodies for that day (addition/unexpected jobs were then added as and when they arrived).

Note: On average, a chauffeur/bearer would attend 3-5 funerals a day and a van crew (normally three people) were expected to 'collect' an average of **10-12** bodies in any one shift (excluding 'call outs' and 'out of hours' pick-ups).

EXHUME/EXHUMATION – The 'digging up' and/or removal of a previously buried body. This can be ordered by a coroner, local council, police, etc., I only had to attend one exhumation during my time as an undertaker and this was done to necessitate the 'moving' of two bodies from one cemetery to another (never did find out why!).

INTERMENT – Another term for a burial.

DOCTORS FORM – In the UK, before a burial/cremation could take place, 'the body' had to be examined by; in the case of a burial **ONE** doctor or; in the case of cremation, **TWO**. Doctors were expected to check for 'sign's of life', etc., (yeah, right!) and were then paid (**£15** was the 'going rate' at the time) for the examination and for signing the form.

CREMATION (CREM) FEES – Payment made to a crematorium authority in exchange for use of their 'services'.

CHALK & LIQUOR – Cockney Slang used by some of my fellow undertakers at the time. Means **VICAR** (or priest, etc.,).

VICAR'S FEE – Payment (around £15 at the time) made to the minister/priest to conduct the funeral service/committal.

MANAGER/SENIOR BEARER – Designated/Appointed undertaker (branch managers would sometimes have arranged the funeral as well) who would be 'in charge' of the funeral 'on the day'. This person would normally return to 'the house' to offer their final condolences (and, of course, to pick-up any tips that may be offered (see 'Box Money' above)).

'SPARE' COFFIN – It was normal practice to carry a 'spare coffin' underneath the plinth (the long section that runs down the middle of the hearse on which the coffin 'sits'). This was a simple 'precaution' just in case of accident/emergency (yep, even undertakers occasionally drop a coffin!). **Note:** Some 'unscrupulous' undertakers would take a 'risk' and 'bung' their 'next job' under here instead (not having to go back to the office/funeral parlour' meant extra 'free time'!).

STOP – Small 'pegs' that were inserted into the holes that 'run along' the plinth (see Spare Coffin above). These were designed to prevent the coffin from moving and fitting them was essential for any hearse driver not wishing to see the coffin smash through the back window when setting off!).

TITFER – Cockney slang for HAT (in the case of the bearers and managers this used to be a Top Hat whereas drivers generally wore a 'chauffeurs' hat (van crew also used to sport rather fetching 'bowler hats' but this practice had been abandoned the year before I started (thank God for that! It was bad enough hearing the 'p-p-p-pick up a Penguin jibes when wearing the 'Monkey Suit' (see next page) but both Mr Benn and those little gits with their 'sifted grains of finer flower' were about in them days too!).

MONKEY SUIT (sometimes called PENGUIN SUIT) – Derogatory term for the top hat and tails worn by an undertaker (personally, I didn't mind wearing one and often thought of myself as a latter day Fred Astaire. Unfortunately though, the hooligans that frequented the various shops and cafes that we occasionally found ourselves in had some *less 'flattering'* comments (if I **never** hear that #@%& p-p-p-pick up a Penguin jibe again it'll be *too soon!*).

E.T. SUIT – Slang term used to describe the protective body suit sometimes worn by van crew when collecting dirty, contagious, etc., bodies. Normally a flimsy, disposable suit with a zip up plastic hood (we also stocked some 'heavier' suits but these were for things like chemical spills and alike and were never carried on the vans (best we could hope for was no mess over our clothes and slightly less smell!). The term derives from the scene in the film *ET* in which scientists wore similar suits.

DIRTY MONEY – Union agreed payment made to staff (van crew) who carried out the collection of 'dirty', rancid, contagious, etc., bodies. **Note:** I received this payment (£35) a total of **3** times (but probably deserved it on many more occasions (the hassle we had to go to in order to claim it was often a deterrent in itself!).

GENUFLECT – A bow/nod offered as a mark of respect for the dead/recently departed. This was often done by the minister/priest conducting the funeral service (and many of the more religious people within a congregation). In *our* case, the manager and bearers would normally genuflect towards the head of the coffin after resting it on the plinth/graveside before committal (see below).

COMMITTAL – The point at which the minister signals for the cremation/burial to be carried out (in the case of a cremation, they would normally press a 'discreet button' (generally hidden under the speakers podium) to indicate to the crematorium staff to close the curtains/and or transport the coffin (in most cases, to the rear of the chapel where the 'ovens' were normally situated).

CORTEGE – Term used to describe the 'procession' of funeral vehicles.

STIFF – A derogatory term used to describe a dead body normally associated with Riga Mortis (see below). The term was frowned on by us of course!

RIGA/RIGA MORTISE – A 'condition' following death where the deceased's body 'stiffens' (often into the most 'peculiar' of contortions!)

and becomes very inflexible. Contrary to common belief, Riga Mortise does **NOT** occur in the majority of deaths (at a rough estimate, maybe 15-30%).

<u>JIP</u> – A 'combination' of puke and excrement! An undertaker's worst nightmare!

Plane Sickening

Background – I had been 'with the Co-op' around 6 months when, to my surprise/horror, I found myself *promoted* to 'Van Crew'. Prior to this I had led a fairly innocuous life learning how to 'outfit' coffins and engrave names of dead people onto little metal coffin-plates! However, this was about to change...

A light plane had crashed
Into a small field
In Kidbrooke, South East London
There were just two travellers;
Husband and Wife

The subsequent report said that
The woman had radioed
That her husband had suffered a heart attack
And that she was
Trying to land the plane in the park by herself
Seeing Sunday morning
Footballers on the ground below
She had aborted her first attempt to land the plane
And, instead, had frantically tried
To land in
The adjacent field which;
Save a small clubhouse, was *empty*

However, she had only very limited flight experience and, in her panic
She had stalled the plane in midair.
Then as the plane turned and pivoted
The engine had **restarted**; *full throttle!*
And dove straight into the ground

It disintegrated on impact!

The Police and Fire-Brigade
Were soon on the scene
And had cordoned off the impact area
From prying, morbid eyes

Down both sides of the long road
Bits of plane and human-being
Were strewn like some kind of
Grotesque Jigsaw puzzle

We arrived an hour or so after the crash
And were beckoned through the cordon
We parked our van by the clubhouse and
Unloaded three shells ready to put *the pieces* in to
We set off back down the road accompanied by several police officers
Whilst fire crews were all around us
Extinguishing the last remnants
Of numerous little fires caused by the explosion and
Leaking aviation fuel

The CAA (Civil Aviation Authority) had just arrived too
And were trying to work-out the best way
To retrieve the engine of the plane
Which had ended up buried many feet below
The muddy ground

We set about the task
Of retrieving the remains of the two occupants of
The now unrecognisable airplane

Carefully we walked along the road and
around twisted, smouldering debris
All three of us spread out a few feet apart
Looking for chalk marks
That had been left by police and fire-crew
Each mark indicating a fragment of skull; dislodged teeth
Bones and other less identifiable 'bits and pieces'

Every now and then
We'd find another piece to add to our gruesome collection

Just to the right of where I was standing
One of the fire-crews had erected a ladder
And a fireman was trying to poke
Part of an arm out of a tree
With a metal pole
All the time we *kept walking; unspoken*

Picking up pieces and
Placing them into carrier bags ready
For the waiting shells

Just then I was approached by a policeman
Who ask me to follow him to the club-house
Near where the plane had crashed

There were numerous tears in the roof
Where plane and torso had ripped through and;
Once inside;
I could see

Part of a *leg* poking out of the open loft

"The caretaker found it"
Said the constable

"He was too shocked to look any further"

I stared up at the ceiling;

A clump of soggy cloth could be seen poking out of the hole
And so I climbed the few steps up the ladder
To collect my *sickening prize*

A large, sodden thigh bone, covered in blood
Was wrapped inside a torn and crumpled trouser leg

I felt something in the pocket as a tightened my grip;

And felt inside to find a wad of money with
an elastic band wrapped around it
I handed it down to the policeman;

"I guess he'll never get to spend **this**!"

He said
With a sad, forced grin and a tinge of sadness in his voice

"I suppose not!"

It seems you **CAN'T** TAKE IT WITH YOU AFTER ALL!"

A few hours later and
We had practically filled the shells
There they sat;
Full of mud, blood, skin and bones

The man and his wife now;

Fully accounted for

The coroner seemed satisfied…

"Any bits left now are either too small to worry about
Or have likely been carried off by the birds or
The local cat population"

*"I guess even death profits **someone**!"*
I thought

We loaded the shells back into the van and
Made our way to the coroner's office
And carried them into the mortuary

We started to pour the jumbled
Contents onto the polished cold slabs
That had seen so much
Death before them

"That's a bit of the woman!"
Said the mortuary attendant

"How the hell can you tell?"
I said

"I just can!
It comes with *experience"*

"This lot's gonna take some putting back together!"
"Still, I reckon I've got the easy job…

The CAA will be down there for **days** collecting
What's left of the plane!"

We finished emptying the shells
Onto the waiting slabs
And viewed the shattered remains of what was;
Just a matter of hours ago;

Two human beings

"It's hard to think of 'that lot' as being something that once
Lived and breathed"
Said Ted

"We're all just flesh and blood mate;
Nothing more than a collection of parts and pieces"

"Yeah, but you don't normally see them spread out
Like the dogs Dinner!" He said

We picked up the empty shells and loaded them back into the van;

"Home?"

I said

"Nah, I reckon we could all do with a pint or two"

"Who's round is it then?"

"Hell, **I'll** buy 'em!
We've just picked up
A hundred quid in overtime"

*"I guess the poor sod **IS** going to be using
Some of that money I found after all!"*

Oh well. Today wasn't a **complete** loss!

We got our beers;

Raised our glasses;

And offered a toast to the
Recently departed

*It was just
Another Sunday lunch-time*

At least for **some** of us!

ON THE FIDDLE

The union had just *re-negotiated* the
Out of hours payments for van crews
And we were now on the promise
Of no less than **3 hours overtime…**

PER BODY!

The Co-op had never had so many people
Wanting to go on the out of hours call out list
(Or so many people praying for plane crashes
Multiple RTA's, plagues and alike!).

It was the first time I'd been *on call*
And so I really didn't know what to expect;

However…
I didn't have to wait long to find out as
The phone rang just before 2AM that morning;

"We've got a 'hit and run' in Peckham"
Said the voice on the end of the phone
"Get your kit on and meet the lads down the yard"…

I stumbled around in the dark looking for my clothes;
(It felt strange putting on a suit and tie at 2AM)
And, having finally clambering into them
|Made my way to the bathroom to freshen up

It took me a while until I was *compos mentis*
But I eventually left the house at around 2.20
And drove the few miles to the depot in Woolwich

I arrived just in time to find Ted opening the shutters and
George backing the *'meat-wagon'* out…

"Erm…Stupid Question"
I said

"But where the hell are we going to take the body
At **this** time in the morning?"

"Watling Street Mortuary of course" Said Ted
"But won't they have closed long ago?"

"Yeah, of course; but we just hop over the wall;
*They leave the key under **the door mat!**"*

(**Note:** in case you're thinking of making a house
call… The place closed years ago!)

*It seemed I had a **lot** to learn…*

George drove us to the scene of the accident
And we were beckoned over to the side of the road by
The waiting ambulance

"The coopers had an urgent call so we hung on for you lot;
There's bugger all else we can do here anyway…

Bloody car FLATTENED him!"

We pulled the van alongside the ambulance and laid the shell down
Beside the body

"Christ!"
Said Ted
As he pulled back the red blanket the ambulance
crew had used to cover the body

"That car must have smashed every bone in his body!"

We lifted the poor chap up and almost
had to 'pour' him into the shell

"He's like one of those *bendy dolls'* my daughter used to play with!"
Commented George

We put the lid back on the shell and walked it back to the Van
And, as the ambulance disappear into the distance,
We did a quick U-Turn and headed off in the opposite direction

Watling Street mortuary was just a mile or two down the road
And was sited in a dark and desolate little side street
With trees all around

"Looks different in the dark'
I said

"Like something out of the **Adams Family!**"

The building, like many of its era
Was a large Victorian structure
With tall intimidating walls and flamboyant brickwork

"I hope you don't think **I'M** climbing over that fence!"
I said looking at the others optimistically

"Well, you **are** the **ROOKIE!**"
Said George

I looked around me searching for any signs of movement

"I wouldn't worry"
Said Ted

"I don't think anyone gives a shit that you're
breaking **into** a mortuary!"

I climbed up on the short wall that ran alongside the front entrance
And pulled myself over the wooden door and finally into the yard"

"#@$%ing Hell!
I can't see a bloody thing!"

"Oh yeah…
You might have wanted to take the ***torch*** over with you!"
Ted chortled

"Thanks Ted, you're a GREAT help!"

Ducking out of the way; the torch came flying over
And landed with a thump in the flower bed to my right

I picked it up and pointed it towards the large
the main gates and turned the
Handle on 'my side'
Before opening them wide

I heard the engine start and George slowly backed the Van in;

The reverse lights
Filled the yard with reddish white light
And just to the right of me
I could make out an old, well worn door mat with just *one word* on it

<u>WELCOME!</u>

(It's funny but, even though I'd been here several times in the past,
I'd never notice either the mat or how 'inappropriate' it was before now!)

I lifted the corner of the mat
And removed a rusty old key from beneath;

"Get the lights on and open the freezer will you;
We'll bring the shell in" shouted Ted

"Keep it down will you… *it's 3 in the morning!*"

"Like anyone *inside* gives a toss!"

I groped inside for the light switch
And felt a re-assuring click followed by a short buzz as
The light bulb flickered on and illuminated the vast
Open room with musty yellow light

As I wandered past the mortuary slabs
To the storage freezers on the left I stopped to ponder;

"*Hmm… I think I fancy Trap Number 3 today!*"
I thought

I opened the door to the freezer and slid the icy cold metal tray out
Ready for our 'hit and run'

Then, just as the tray locked into position;
The early morning stillness was *suddenly* interrupted by;

The dulcet sound of a
Lone fiddle player!

I froze on the spot!
(And it wasn't due to my proximity to the mortuary fridge!)
As I felt a tingling down my neck and spine
And a uneasy dryness in my throat…

"Is that… **YOU**… Ted???"
"I've seen **Young Frankenstein** before you know!
This **isn't** going to work!"

The fiddle player played on…

"It's not #@&%ing funny you pillark!"

As I continued cursing and cussing…

The music got louder and louder until;
Without warning;

It suddenly

STOPPED!

I sighed with relief and
Was just about to put it down to a passing car radio
When, to my utter horror and disbelief…

An *eerie female voice* started echoing around the room…

"I hope you enjoyed that one!!!" she said

(NOW I *KNEW* it **wasn't** Ted!)

"Erm… Yes… it was…Erm… *very nice*…"
I said (trying not to sound too petrified)

"Let me have your next requests!"
She demanded

"Look… I don't know what your game is but
There are **THREE** of us you know!"

Just then, as if on queue
Ted and George appeared with the shell and
At almost the very same moment…

The voice… STOPPED!

"What was that?"
Said Ted looking somewhat puzzled
"It sounded like you were *talking* to someone?"

Before I could answer him;
The mortuary suddenly filled with the unmistakable sound of…

THE 1812 OVERTURE!
(Complete with CYMBALS and CANNON FIRE!)

"Jesus Christ, who the #@%$ is that?"
Screamed Ted
Dropping the shell (and its unfortunate occupant)
Right onto George's left foot

"OWWWW, YOU PRATT!!!!!"
Shouted George
(Just as another cannon salvo went off)

Holding his crushed size 9 in one hand
George then started hoping around the
mortuary like a demented frog in a suit
In almost perfect time with the composition now reaching a crescendo

"Thank God **YOU** can hear it too"
I said

"I thought I was #@&%ing losing it!"

Ted and I slowly walked forward and towards the haunting melody
(Leaving George hopping up and down beside the cracked shell)

"I heard someone playing the #@%$ing **violin** earlier!"
I whispered
My voice now trembling in fear

"Don't panic"
Said Ted
Trying his best to reassure me

"There's got to be a *logical reason* behind all this"

"Yeah, right…
Someone's sneaked Yehudi Menuin and a 30 piece orchestra
Into a #@%$ing mortuary at 3 o'clock in the morning;
Sounds perfectly #@%$ing logical to me!"

Half trembling;
Half laughing; at the ludicrousness of what I'd just said

We approached the rear of the mortuary
Where the sound seemed to be *at it's loudest*

In the distance we could see a large wooden table
Resting in the shadow of the frosted glass window
That dominated the end wall
And, on the table…

We could make out a faint glow

"Blimey! Would you Adam and Eve it!"
"It's a bleedin' radio!"
Shouted Ted
In his best Cockney Accent
(Well, best for *him*, given that he'd live all his life in **Woolwich**!)

Sure enough;
A big old bakelite box was sitting there on the table
And, as we focused in
We could see an old twisted brown mains cord
Winding its way from the back of the box
And up into the light socket above

"It's an old **valve** job!"
"It must have come on when you flipped the light switch and slowly
Come to life"

"Great!"
I said
"Here we are in a old mortuary in the early hours of the morning and;

"Something **COMES TO LIFE!**
That's bloody thing's taken **10 years** off my life!"

"I didn't know what the hell to think…
I thought Glen #@&%ing Miller had come back to haunt me!"

**"ANY CHANCE WE COULD GET THIS
#@&%ING STIFF IN THE #@&£ING FREEZER!"**
Shouted George
(Who had been watching on with painful distain)

"I've already broken my #@&%ing foot!
Is it asking too much if we could try and get home before
I die *of old age* too?"

"Oooohh…"
Smiled Ted
"Someone got out of the *wrong side of the
bed* this morning didn't they!"

"I'll give you wrong side of the #@&%ing bed"
"I've got a good mind to report you for **industrial injury!**"

Ted and I wandered back over to the shell
(Which was still lying on the floor next to George)
Lifted it up and carried it over to
Trap Number 3…

"I bet my #@&$ing foot looks like him now!"

Said George
Viewing the mangled body as we slid it onto the metal tray

"*You What?*
Said Ted

"Your foot looks like a *16 stone mangled West Indian?*"
Trying to wind him up even further

"Just get on with it will you;
I've got a cold bed and a **hot woman** to get home to!"

"Wife got **flu** again"
Retorted Ted (pushing his luck one more time!)

"Right, ***THAT'S IT…***
You can #@%£ing drive now!"

"It's your fault that I can't move my toes any more
So the least you can do
Is drive the bloody van back to the depot"

"*Yeah, yeah…*
Anything for a ***cripple!***"

Smiled Ted

"I suppose *I've* got to jump over the
#@&%ing fence again?"

I said

"Well, you are…"

"Yeah, I know…
the #@%$ing **rookie**…"

I switched off the lights
And closed the door to
The fading echo of
Little Brown Jug
Before slipping the old rusty key
Back under the Mat once more

Clambering back over the door and into the road
I looked back into the darkness and smiled;

*"This'd make a good story if I ever **wrote a book**"*
I though

Ted and George
Were patiently waiting for me in the van…

"That was fun!"
Said Ted

"It's not often you get a **serenade** at 3 in the morning!"
He smiled

"Yeah, right!
I'm *still* shaking even now!"

"I know how to *relax* you"

Smirked Ted

"What say I…

Put the **RADIO** on!"

Me in the 'monkey suit' - circa 1976

☺

MANS BEST FRIEND

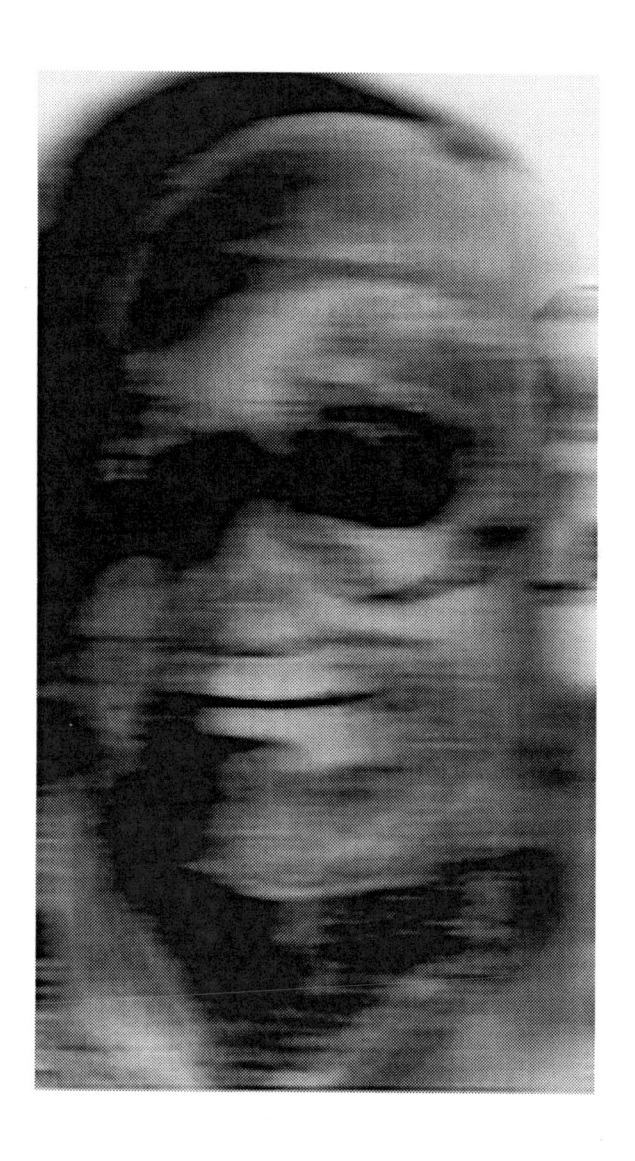

We arrived in Greenwich a few minutes after getting *the call*

The house was situated
On a busy main road
Complicated further by a steep hill

The Police were waiting for us when we arrived
And directed us to park our van
In front of the police car

We were then led to Number 22
By a young constable

"I'll leave you to it"
He said

"I don't envy you <u>this</u> one"

(I could tell by the way that he said it that
We were going to regret turning up!)

Another policeman stood at the door;

"The coroner's nearly finished"
He said

"You'll find him in the second room on the right…"

It was a typical;
'Old persons' house…

Dank, dusty and full of old Brick-a-brack
Ancient faded pictures of
People in uniform
Lined the right-hand wall
And an old blue melamine table
Sat in the corner of the kitchen

With an open jar of marmite
And some mouldy bread lying on it

AND THEN ***IT*** HIT US ...

A strong, *revolting* stench
That you more **tasted** than smelt

My stomach turned as I tried to hold my breath

"We're gonna need the masks, possibly even the E.T. Suits!"
I said

As I breathed in again
The vile stench overpowered me
And I ran outside and involuntarily deposited
The contents of my stomach over the rear balcony

The young Policeman looked up;

"See what I mean"
He said

A few moments later and we were back in the house
Paper masks over faces and ready *for almost anything;*

"These things don't help much"
I said

*"I've found some of the old fella's
Aftershave and armpit sprays"*
Ted said as he entered the room behind me

"Well for Christ sake start sprinkling it around will you!"
"I don't wanna lose my stomach **again!**"

Oddly enough; the smell of Old Spice and Brut 33
Seemed to make the smell… **WORSE!**
But it least it was just enough to make it;
Tolerable

We went in to the lounge
Where the old boy was lying by the window;
The coroner was stood just to the left of him;

"Bit of a stinker, ay, fellers?"

"You're not kidding!"
I mumbled through the mask

"You think the SMELL'S bad;
You wait 'til you *turn him over!*"

Warily, we moved closer and could see that
Loose chunks of flesh;
Rotten and putrid
Were lying all around like bits of
Discarded Turkish Delight

Turning him over, we were greeted with the sight that
Half his face has been *eaten away* and
A great 'gaping hole' could be seen
With a partly gnawed shoulder blade protruding out if it!

"Poor old chap must have collapsed weeks ago.
*I reckon his **dogs** had him for **dinner**!*"

The RSPCA had
Taken the dogs away to be destroyed
(Although by all accounts they were on their last legs anyway)

The smell
We discovered
Was; *part rotting flesh;*
Part dog excrement

Which we could now see was strewn all over the room
Along with a selection of small bones
And tiny splatters of blood

The old fella lying there;
In amongst it all;
Covered in bite marks

Doggy dinner for two!

I'm glad now that I had thrown up *earlier*
As there nothing left for having seen the sight

We put on our rubber gloves
And carefully peeled the putrid body off the floor
And away from the rancid, blood soaked carpet
Which was *alive with maggots*

The right-hand side of his face was literally;
Eaten away

"Dogs don't normally eat *human* flesh"
Explained the coroner

"They must have been starving to death to do something
Like **THIS**"

"Still, they're paying 'the ultimate price' now for feasting on
Forbidden Fruit"

FRUIT! I thought

Definitely **NOT** the word I would have used!

We peeled the last bit of him off the carpet and
Moved towards the waiting shell;

As we moved, I could feel the sticky, tacky skin
Even through the gloves
And the stench as we lifted him free from the carpet
Nearly brought up 'the reserves'
From my aching stomach

"Got any more of that awful bloody aftershave?"
I said

Staring into the half-eaten face;
Stubble one side
Teeth marks on the other
I found myself thinking…

*"I'm glad I've only got a **CAT**!"*

"Don't worry about the carpet;
The council are on their way
To fumigate the place"

"Great"
I thought
"It's a shame they couldn't have done it **BEFORE** we'd arrived!"

"Oh well, for what its worth
I'm going to put us in for **dirty money**
For this one!" said George

"Well, woopy #@%£ing doo!"

"I'm going have to burn these bloody clothes when I get back
And it took me **weeks** to get the last lot from supplies!"

26

We bundled the old fella up
And unceremoniously heaved the shell up and over
The balcony and into the van below

At that precise moment…

A DOG RAN PAST!

And I felt a tingle run down my spine

Man's best friend
I thought

Not THIS time!

WENT TO PIECES

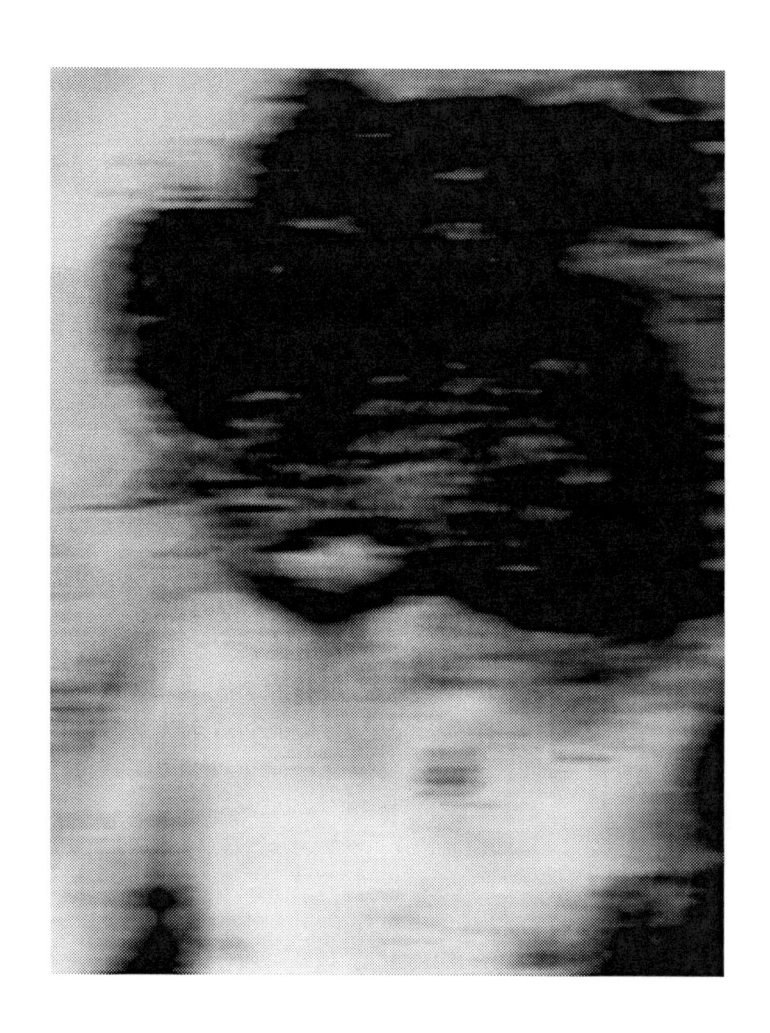

It's not often I got a *local call;*
Most of the time
We'd be up in SE London
Or further out
It's just the way things went

However, this particular night
The call came in to say that
There had been a *suicide* at a house just 'up the road' to where I lived

This was a *result!*

As, by the rules of our '*verbal agreement'
If one of the crew
Lived within walking distance to the 'pick up'
Then they could meet the others there
(Thus saving the trip to Woolwich and back)

* It was necessary to keep this as a 'verbal' agreement
So that we could still claim the mileage
allowance and travel time of course!

As it happens;
I *drove* the half a mile or so to the address that I had been given
(I suppose that I could have walked but
Even in 'those days' we'd picked up
More than our fair share of people who had
Just walked up the road but
Hadn't come back again!)

As I arrived the police and coroner
Were standing at the front door *talking;*

"It's a pretty **messy** *affair*"
The coroner said as I approached

"But we'll need **all** the 'bits' and pieces I'm afraid so
You'd best wait until the fire-brigade return with the **ladder**"

LADDER?
Strange I thought;
Until I walked *inside;*

There in front of me
Sitting in a tattered old chair
Was the body of a man;
Completely butt naked and
Covered in blood
With one notable and obvious;
Problem

HIS FACE WAS <u>MISSING</u>!

On the floor in front of him
In a pool of blood and membranes
Lay a shotgun and an empty shell casing

From his neck upwards
Save a small piece of chin and jawbone;

Nothing remained

Now the reason for the ladder became obvious…

To be honest
I don't think the poor sod
Had thought about this for one moment but…
When he had rested the barrel of the shotgun
Under his chin and pulled the trigger

And, at the point where his cranium shattered
And his brains sprayed out across the room
He **SHOULD** have realised that…

WHITE POLYSTYRENE CEILING TILES
Were <u>NOT</u> the best places to 'deposit ones features!'

Now; looking high above me; I could see
A crimson **kaleidoscope**
Made up of bone, blood and ceiling tile
Forming a sort of red
'Join-the-dots' affair
That wouldn't have looked out of place on Blue Peter

"#@%&ing Hell"
I thought to myself…

"What a mess!"

As I was admiring the Pollock-esque patterns
Now indelibly weaved into the ceiling tiles;

My two companions finally arrived

"#@%&ing Hell"
"What a mess!"

"You don't **REALLY** expect us to
Climb up there and pries that lot off the ceiling do you?"

"We're undertakers not archaeologists!"

The coroner looked at us with a cold glare;

"We pay the Co-op to collect bodies and, unless I'm mistaken
That lot up there comes under that heading"

Graham couldn't resist himself…

"HEADING!"
He said

"Are you trying to be funny?"
Sadly… **He wasn't!**

"As I was saying…" he continued

That lot up there
ALL needs to be bagged up
With the rest of him;
Every little bit is; *evidence*."

Resigned to our task
We all took *turns* up the ladder
Wandering round the room with it like
Some demented Come Dancing Team
*(If only we'd brought the
Top Hat and Tails!)*

"'Ere, they were doing something like this on
Last weeks
'It's a Knockout!'"
Said Ted

"I'll #@&% knock **YOU** out in a minute!"

"Just get on with it will you!
I'm fed up holding this bloody ladder"

Scraping bits of bone
Sinew, eyeball and teeth
Out from the high ceiling tiles
With a rusty old penknife
Wasn't exactly what I had planned
For my evening

Putting up with Ted's
Stand-up-comedian routine
Wasn't either!

We finally extracted the last 'piece'
Though, by now,

It had taken us best part of 2 hours to
Collect it all
(Plus half the ceiling tiles too in the event!)

"Some 'quick job' this has turned out to be"
I said

By the time the others set off
Back to the coroners court;

Not only had I missed

'The last pint'

But I have to say that I'd also been put off of using
White Polystyrene Ceiling Tiles

FOREVER!

Oh yeah…

One last word of advice…

If **YOU** ever contemplate
Committing suicide *yourself…*

Might I suggest that you …

Take an overdose…

IT'S A LOT LESS MESSY!

MAGGOTS!

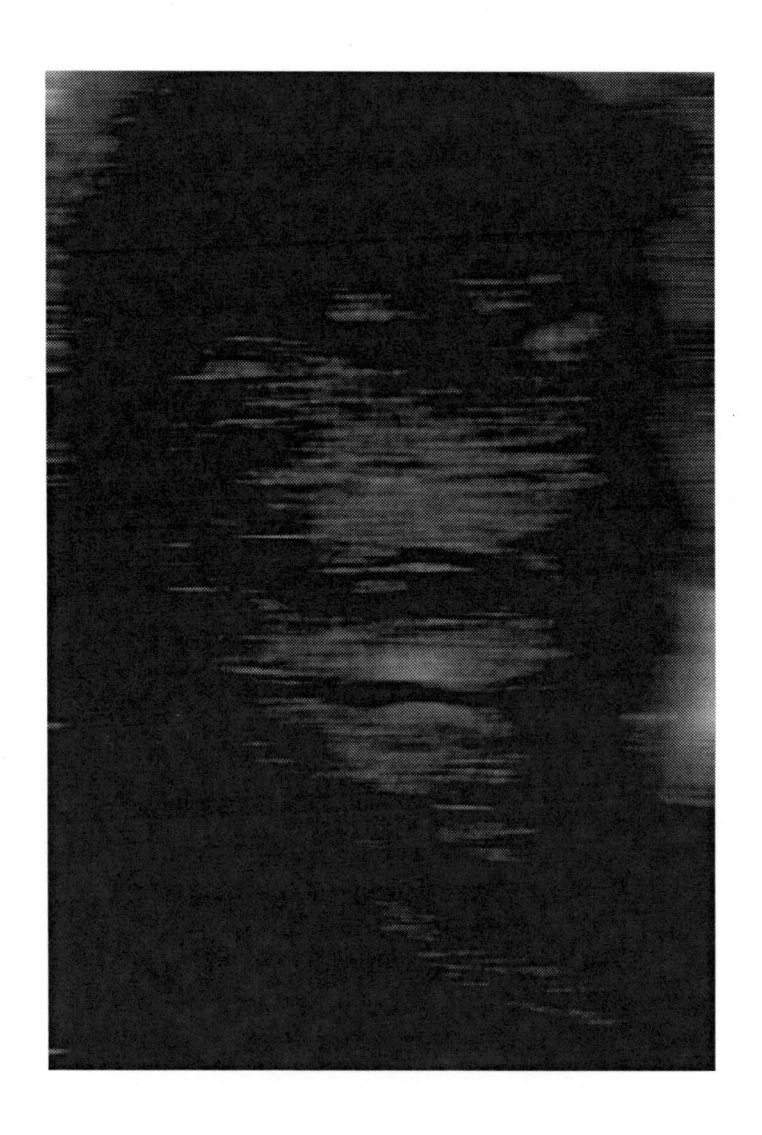

The call came for a pickup
Just up the road from our Head Office (Woolwich)
We could have walked it
Had we not needed the van
To carry the shell

It was an upstairs flat in a Block of Maisonettes;
An old fella;
Been dead *some time* we were told

When we arrived
The police were still there
But the coroner had already left

"Better hurry up"
Said the policeman at the door

"The public health people will be here soon
To gut this place and clean it up"

We walked down the passageway
And into the lounge
Where the body lay

In front of us;
Face down and lying on his side
Lay the old man
His body was bent and lying 'banana shaped'
In front of an old gas fire
He was wearing a faded tartan dressing gown
And white linen pyjamas
His slippers were stained brown with age

As we neared the body
And ventured over to the fire where he was lying
With his face to the floor

We could see from the colour/texture of his skin
That there was 'something unusual' about it

Most noticeably;
Despite the fact that he was an old *white* man
Most of the skin that we could see
Was a mottled brown colour
Layered with wrinkles and almost
Leather-like in appearance

We heard a voice at the door
It was the policeman…

"He collapsed a couple of weeks ago"
"Right there in front of the fire.
He's been *'cooking away'* ever since!"

"What's the deal with the carpet?"
I said

It's like walking on *a sponge cake*

"Oh, yeah, I forgot to mention…

IT'S **SWARMING** WITH MAGGOTS!

Literally thousands of the little buggers
Most of them are under the carpet
Or on the old boy himself"

"Rubber glove time!"
I declared

Sadly, there wasn't much left
Of the old boy when we turned him over
Most of the flesh was scorched and
Riddled with maggot marks

Eyes; tongue; cheeks;
They were all putrid and blistered
There must have been hundreds
Of maggots crawling around inside him;
Eating him from *within*

The irony was that most of the
Burnt and charred skin around his face which was
Closest to the fire when he fell
Was still 'relatively intact'
Having harden and become impervious
To the maggots

We scooped his body up like an old rag doll
And lowered him into the shell
Maggots and all

We wandered back across the squishy carpet
And back down the stairs to the cab

"Bung him on the rear slab"
Said the coroner when we arrived

"He's really chucking up"
I said
"Maggot Smorgasbord"

"Not to worry; I'm used to it"

The empty shell was still heaving with maggots
And they were now all over everything (and everyone) else too!

We slid the old fella onto the slab and then
Washed the shell out with boiling water

"Here, the little buggers are swimming in it!
They think it's a bloody **Jacuzzi**!"

"Boiling water wont 'get 'em'
"Use the **acid**!
It's the only way to kill 'em"

Sure enough
One glug of the foul smelling liquid
(Used to clean the congealed blood off the slabs)
And the 'movement' soon

Stopped

We rinsed the shell out
With hot water once more
And cleaned ourselves up

As we were walking back to the van
Ted spotted a couple of maggots

*Crawling **out** of the pool of liquid*

And away to ***freedom**!*

Maggots…

I thought

TOUGH LITTLE BASTARDS!

The Route of All Evil!

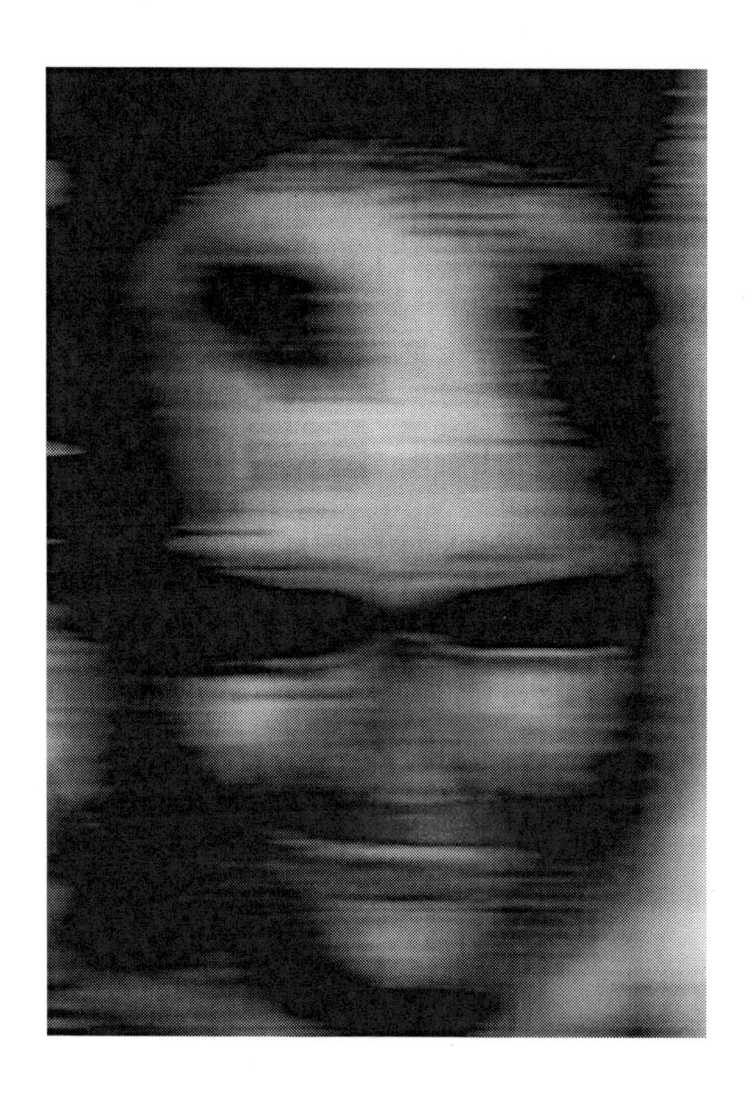

It was a nice sunny Sunday morning.

The call came in around 9AM and we were
soon to end up at a quaint little
'Out of the way cottage' in the heart of the Kent countryside

We knew that something *'special'* had happened
When we were told to bring **FOUR** shells with us and were then
Met by a police escort as we neared the house

When we arrived, the whole area was one big police cordon
And there were blue flashing lights *everywhere*

There was a police helicopters hovering
overhead and we could see another
Away in the distance

As we drove down the long driveway towards the front of the cottage
It looked like the **whole** of the Kent Police force were there too!

*The **County** Coroner met us at the door;*
(Now we REALLY knew something 'REALLY big' had happened
(Normally, we'd only ever glimpse the county coroner
at the coroners office or in court and he almost never
ventured out this far (let alone on a **Sunday morning**!)

"Gentlemen…" He said
You had better prepare yourself for a bit of a heartbreaker'

"We've got a **whole family** in here that have been
Tied up, tortured and killed
The youngest daughter is just
5 years old!"

As we walked towards the hallway
The splintered front door was our first glimpse of
The carnage that awaited us inside

There was a huge mirror lying shattered in the hallway and
Pieces of broken furniture and ornaments scattered along its length

We followed the county coroner into a large
room bathed in sunshine and there
Inside;
Trussed up like *grotesque chickens*;
Were the bodies of three people…
1 woman and 2 young girls

All three had their hands tied behind their backs and
Were slumped and lifeless on the huge ornate
carpet that dominated the room which
Was soaked in blood and bore witness to the
tragedy that had befallen them

The woman was in her late thirties and was
wearing a pink flannelette dress
With a huge tear at one side;
And a crimson blood stain down the front

A neat hole in her forehead was caked in congealed blood
Which had dripped onto the carpet earlier and made
Morbid little patterns on the floor

As we looked around, we could see that they had **ALL** been
Shot through the head!

The two girls were huddled together near the
huge fire at the end of the room
Which was still glowing with untended embers

A stream of blood led from the bodies and across the carpet
To the wall on the other side

The youngest girls arm looked like it had been torn out of its socket
And was swollen and black with bruising and red with clots

Both girls were wearing identical yellow pyjamas
With little teddy bear emblems on the fronts
That were now almost complete obscured by bloody stains

*"The **father's** upstairs"*
The coroner said

"If you think **THESE** are bad;
You should see **this** poor chap!"

I left my colleagues downstairs to start bagging the three females and
Followed the coroner upstairs and in to
A small, dimly lit room off to the right

I could just make out the silhouette of a man
Slumped in the corner of the room

The coroner turned the light on;

Resting against the wall was a large
Barely recognizable body of a middle aged man

Naked from the waist up his torso was covered with
So many cuts and bruises
It was almost impossible to distinguish his features

I stared in disbelief at this tragic figure and
Looked upon his face with anguish;

His left eye was swollen like a jacket potato whilst
His right eye was wide open and filled with blood

To the right of his cut and puffy mouth
Part of his cheek bone could be seen
Jutting out through the battered flesh
Like a half-eaten stick of seaside rock

Most of his bottom teeth had been pushed through the skin
(Presumably by some kind of blow to the head)
And were now sticking out of his face
Just below his lips

I say **MOST** of his teeth as several more could be seen
Lying on the floor, floating in the puddle of blood
Emanating from his twisted body

One look at him and you just KNEW that...

Whatever happened...

Death must have been one hell of a *relief* to him.

I couldn't comprehend what could possible motivate anyone to do *this*
To another human being

Of course, as it eventually turned out the
motivation in *this* case was, of course ...

GREED!

The poor chap in front of me was apparently
A respected businessman and was known locally as
A bit of a *wheeler dealer*

Mistakenly
THEY thought that he'd have
Some of his fortune hidden at **home**

A fortune in jewellery or perhaps even
A SAFE

Little had they realised as they tortured these poor souls that
The mirror in the hallway
Now shattered and lying in pieces

Had been worth thousands of pounds or that
The blood stained carpet had come all the way for Persia and
Was worth a Kings Ransom to the right dealer

NO!
They wanted **CASH**
And they killed each and every one of them trying to get it
Before finally taking out their frustration on anything they could

The house was a mess
Furniture and paintings smashed and destroyed
Ancient treasures gone;
FOREVER

"There's a fortune here in antiques"
Said the coroner

"But they only had a few hundred in *cash*"

"Four lives lost forever;

For the sake of few hundred quid!"

We bagged the four of them up and
One at a time
Took them back to the van

"The county coroner will be here for a while yet
But one of his deputies is waiting for you at the mortuary"
The policeman said

As we drove away from the cottage and
Back down the winding driveway we were all
Silent

I just kept thinking of those poor people
And what sort of ***animals***

Could have done that to them

But, then again…

ANIMAL

Seemed like *too good a word* for them…

At least animals kill;
Because they **HAVE** to!

As we left the coroners court
Ted looked at me and said

*"I'm glad **I'm** not rich"*

*"Do I take it that it's my round **AGAIN** then?"*

I replied

Made me Jump

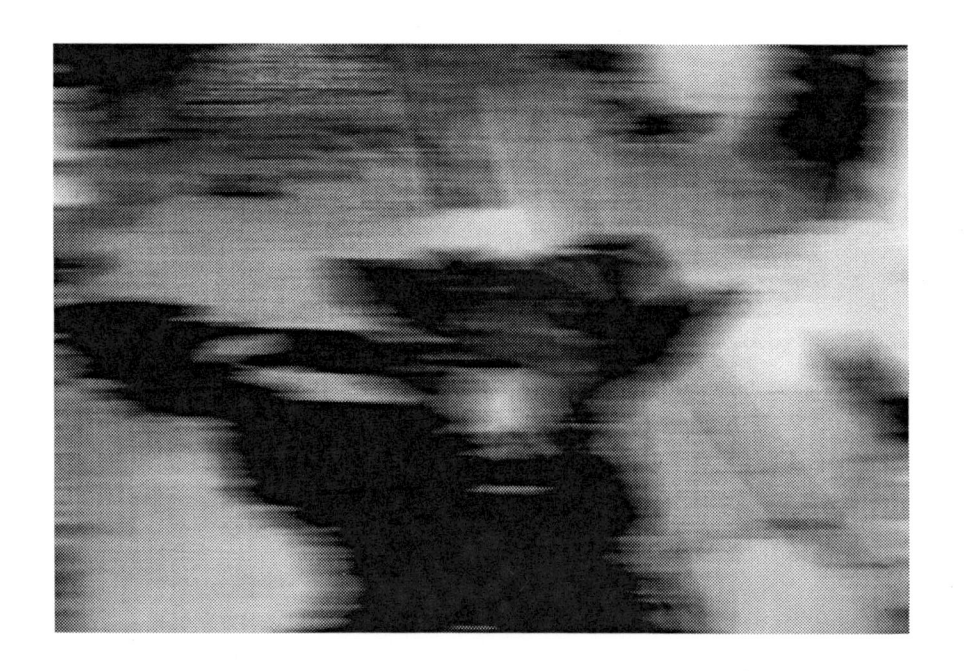

Dad and I were sitting watching the TV
on a typical Sunday afternoon

Charlton had just scored a goal and the smell of roast
potatoes wafted through our little 8th floor flat

We'd lived in the block of flats for nearly seven years now
It was OK and the view was reasonable enough

Of course, there was no 'neighbourhood' as such

Despite being 15 floors high these places were nothing more
Than a bunch of *'little boxes'*
Locking up the occupants and locking out the world.

We'd probably seen our next door neighbours
TWICE *in all those years!*

Charlton were 'on the move again' when,
suddenly and without warning a
'Large human shaped figure' came hurtling past the window!

Dad and I just looked at each other for a second and
Then I got up and looked out of the window;

There, right in the middle of the resident's car park was
The figure of *a body!*

"Ring for an ambulance!"
I shouted

"I'm going down to check it out!"

I rushed to the lift, which seemed to take forever to arrive
And frantically pushed the button for the ground floor

As I exited the lift I could see through the open door;
A body, dressed in a brown dressing gown
Half **embedded** in the concrete

Blood was oozing in **all** directions

"*On reflection*" I thought;
"Getting Dad to call for an **ambulance** might have been a
Tad optimistic!"

I walked over to the lifeless body and saw that it was
The body of a young woman

I looked up and could see a few people
starring out of the window's of their
Little Boxes and could hear voices mumbling from above

Dad appeared with a blanket under his arm and I covered her up
Having at once realised that there was little else we could do

By now, several other 'curious' people had appeared
And one old chap suggested that we try *the kiss of life!*

"*I'm no medic*"

I said

"But, *trust me…*

I know a thing or two about *death* and this poor sod is going to need
a whole lot more than a *kiss* to get her back up on her feet again!"

I few minutes later the ambulance arrived
and I recognised one of the crew;

"Well, it's not often you get a call **THIS** close to home huh!"

He said

"I take it it's one for *US* rather than you lot"

I said

Realising that I'd rather stated the obvious

"I have no idea who she was
She just came hurtling past the window a few minutes ago"

By now, quite a crowd had started to assemble
But no-one seemed to recognise the poor women

"What a bloody awful way to go!"

Dad remarked.

"Is there a **GOOD** way then?"

"Oh, you know what I mean…
I mean; Look at her…
She must only be about 20 years old"

The ambulance crew radioed in as the Police arrived;

"Anyone see what happened?"

"Well…
We didn't really see *a lot* other than
The poor woman hurtle past our 8th floor window"
I said

They took our names and address and said that
They'd be up to take a statement shortly

"Thanks mate, can you leave it to us now"

Said one of them

And so we made our way back to our
Cold Sunday lunches

A few minutes later the phone rang…

"We've got a jumper!"
Said the voice

"I know mate'
I'm **already** on the case!"

When Ted arrived in the van a few minutes later
I beckoned him over and told him what had happened

"You lucky b*stard" He said
"Why won't they kill themselves on **my** doorstep!
I never get any *breaks!*"

The policeman I'd spoken to earlier walked over to us

"We found this *pair of slippers*"
He said
We're pretty sure that they belonged to *her*

"Funny thing is…
From the people we've spoken to so far
It seems that she jumped from the *12th* floor landing

But we found the slippers in the corridor on the *10th* floor

*From all accounts she must have stopped to
change her shoes on the way up
Before jumping!"*

"Strange"

I said
"I wonder what she must have been thinking"

Ted looked at the slippers and then looked back at me;

"Typical" He said

"What is?"

"Just my luck; these are only size **4's…**

***The missus could have done with another
Pair of decent slippers!"***

Me trying a coffin for size - circa 1975

All Salted

It was around three in the afternoon
And we had just got back to the yard

We had a couple of 'Hospital pick-ups' left and that was it for the day

Just then the foreman walked up to us;
"Sorry lads; we've just got a 'house-call' for you!"

We were told that it was an old man
Who had been **ill** for *some time* and who passed away a couple of hours ago

The house was a few minutes up the road

When we arrived, the old fella's niece was waiting for us;

I made *the introductions* and left the others to bring the shell in

The niece didn't seem too upset as she beckoned me in

"You were quick" she said
"We were only up in Woolwich, Madam"
I replied

She led us up a thin, dark passageway
And up a dusty staircase to a small bedroom

"Before we go in" She said

"I'd best *warn* you'
He's been *unwell* for some time and…

Well, he's made *a **bit of a mess!***"

As we entered the room
There was a heavy *Shitty smell*
And the ripe smell of something
We undertakers call
'Jip'

However, the smell was NOTHING
Compared to the *sight…*

Looking around us
We could see that the entire room was *splattered*
In dark, brown stains

There didn't seem to be an area of wall or
Floor that wasn't affected

Even the **CEILING** had a few marks on it!

We stared at each other for a few seconds
Before finally regaining our composure

And then we all turned to look at the niece hoping
For a word of
Explanation

"Yes" She Said
"I'm really sorry about the mess"

"Only… he's spent the last few months
on **SALTS!**"

As she turned to leave the room an *irrepressible smirk*
Started to appear on Frank's (the 'joker in the pack') face;

That was it
Looking first at the walls and then back at us and
Without missing a beat he says...

"**SALTS! SALTS!**
Look at this...
She must have meant #@&% SOMER-**SALTS!**"

Now, there are many professions
Where the act of *uncontrollable laughter*
May seem 'wholly inappropriate'
An **undertaking** is at the top of the list

But, at this point
Ted and I frankly lost it completely
(Indeed, we would probably been rolling on the floor
Had it not been completely covered in...!)

Fearing that the niece might still be in earshot
We did our very best to stifle the laughter
But the combination of the 'impromptu' comment
And the smell of Sprinkled excrement
Left us gasping for breath for several
Excruciating minutes
Before we both finally managed to regain
Sufficient composure to at least try and carry out our sombre duty"

Frankly;

How we managed to get the old chap into the shell
And down the stairs without causing

Serious offence

To the dearly departed's kith and kin
Is quite beyond me
But we *somehow* managed to portray the persona
Of the consummate professions
Long enough to pull it off

I proffered our condolences
And bid our farewells
Before finally falling back into the Van
For one last bout of laughter

As we pulled away from the house
I leaned past Ted and looked over to Frank
Who was sitting there as unemotional as ever…

"*Sometimes Frank*"

"You really #@%£ing liability!"

The Axe-Man Cometh

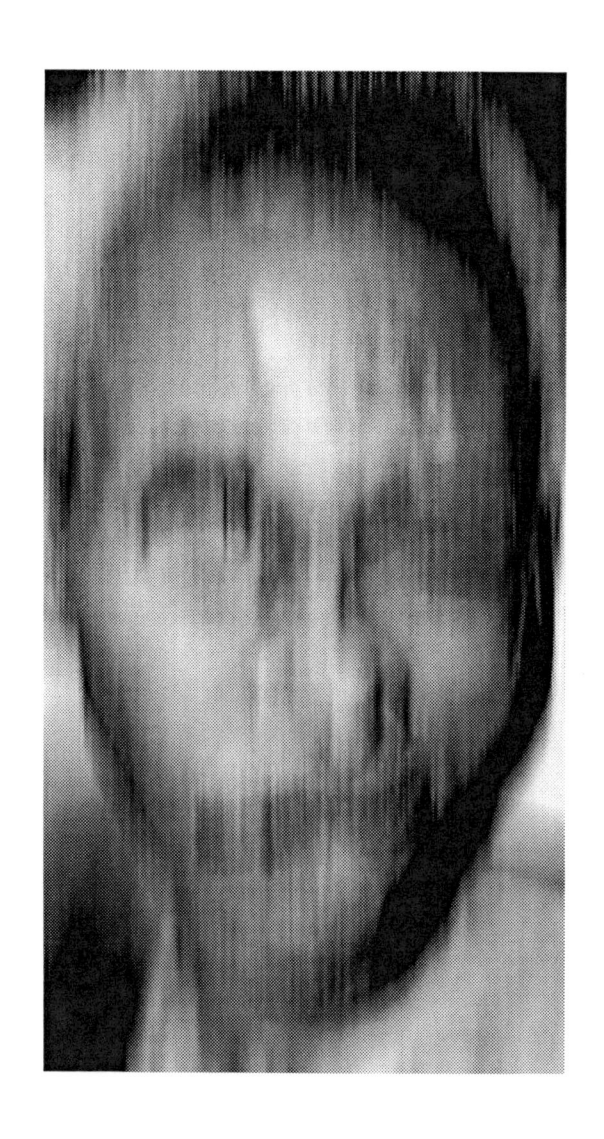

It was a freezing cold December morning when,
At just after 2AM, the phone started ringing….
"There's been a murder in New Cross"
Said the voice
"Meet you at HQ in 30 minutes"

Another 'lovely assignment for a half-asleep undertaker!

At least, at two in the morning, the roads to
Woolwich were completely empty so,
For a change, the drive in took just *10 minutes*

When I arrived, Ted and Graham were already there
(And, for another nice change, I wasn't the
designated *driver* that night either!)

The Van flew down the road, through Charlton and we arrived in
New Cross some 15 minutes later

There were a couple of police cars outside the house and
The coroner was just pulling up outside

A few neighbours were also standing around
trying to 'get in on the act'
But we ignored everyone as usual and went to speak to
The policeman at the front gate;

"Hi chaps. The forensic guys are just finishing up;
If you can wait just inside the door, they'll tell you when you can
Do your thing"

We waited about 10 minutes and were then
escorted along the short corridor
And through to the rear of the house into
the kitchen where the victim lay

He was a large coloured chap in his mid-
twenties and he was lying in a
Pool of blood by the kitchen fridge

Beside him was a large axe with blood stains on the handle and blade

"Bag the axe up will you"
Said the coroner to the policeman who had led us in

"You can have the body in a sec chaps, we're nearly done here."

"I take it the axe was the murder weapon?"
I said stating the obvious once more

"Almost certainly but I'll make up my mind
for sure after I've examined it.

In the meanwhile, try and mind his head, there's two dirty
great chunks taken out of it and it's still dripping blood

Best hurry too… the guy who did this is
still supposed to **be in the area!**
We've got officers out searching for him now"

He didn't have to ask **TWICE!**

The others went to get the shell whilst I covered
the poor sods head with a towel and wrote out the
body label with the details I'd been given

The coroner waved a cheery 3AM goodbye and left me to it

Just as I had knelt down to attach the body label to his big toe…

The back door suddenly and violently swung open!

In about *half a nano-second* I was off up
the corridor like Roger Bannister
Screaming for all I was worth that
The murderer had returned to the scene of the crime

As I flew down the corridor like some demented idiot
I envisaged the axe raised and poised at the back of my head

But I never turned round to check!

As I approached the front door still screaming at the top of my voice
Two huge burley coppers came flying in almost knocking me flat!

"WHERE THE HELL IS HE???"

They shouted

*"I think he's still in the kitchen…
You can catch him if you're quick!"*

I spun around and took up position

BEHIND THEM!

As they burst in to the kitchen I could see;
(Over their shoulders, naturally!)…

My two colleagues standing there
Smirks as wide as he Thames
Holding their chests with laughter
And pointing at me
Hiding behind the two coopers
Looking as pale as the fridge door!

"Oh, funny #@££ing ha, ha!"

I swore

"I nearly had a #@%$ing heart attack!"

The two policemen
Now with broad smiles on their faces
Turned around to look at me
And joined in the laughing

"That's cheered me up no end!"

Said one of them

"I haven't had a good laugh like that in ages!"

Ice-Cream at Night!

Ted rang;

"We've got a call and they've told us to load up…"

'BIG BERTHA!'

"Oh **crap**!" I thought
Instant Hernia time again!

We loaded up the van and set off for a downstairs
flat just outside Abbey Wood

A man in a thick brown dressing gown came
out to greet us as we pulled up;

"Hi fella's;
Thanks for getting here so soon

How many of you are there?"

"*Three* of us" I replied

"Oh dear… I don't think that's going to be **enough!**"

He beckoned us in and led as along a dimly lit hallway and
Into a 'makeshift' downstairs bedroom

As I entered the room the first thing I noticed was
Piles of plastic plates and huge, family sized Ice-Cream tubs
Scattered all over the room;

"***She's*** *been bed-ridden for years*"
Explained the husband

"**EATING** was her only joy;

She **_loved_** ice-cream

She'd eat tubs of the stuff
I didn't have the heart to deny her
It was her only *real pleasure* in life."

Our eyes turned to the middle of the room and to the
King-Sized bed that took pride of place

Lying on it, sheets pulled to one side,
Was the most *gigantic woman* I had ever seen!

She was wearing a colossal yellow nightdress which, at first glance
I had mistaken for the quilt cover

I never even realised that you could buy garments of such titanic scale
But the proof was right there in front of us

The poor chap looked embarrassed as we desperately tried to hide
Our expressions of disbelief and abstract Horror

"I told the chap at the funeral place that he needed to send *more men*"
He said

"Not to worry Sir, we're used to dealing with such 'situations'
I relied reassuringly

By all means make yourself comfortable and
We'll give you a call when we're 'done'!"

After he'd left, we wandered over to the bed and tried
To 'Size up' our options;

"There's **no way** she's going to fit in Big Bertha!"
Said Ted

"I mean… **Look at her…**

Her **thigh's** bigger than my **WAIST** for Christ sake and she's got
TWO of 'em"

We called for another van crew!

In the meanwhile, we pondered just HOW on earth
We were going to get her out of the room

"I reckon the corridor ought to be wide-enough
But she's going to be a real bugger to get through the bedroom door!"

Oh well, we thought
Let's at least try to get her off the bed for now;

"Sod that' I said
"We'd never be able to get our arms underneath her let alone
Get a strong enough grip to lift her off"

"OK then…Let's take the **mattress** and all"
Suggested Ted

A little after 11PM the other crew arrived and seemed as
Perplexed as us at the conundrum before them;

"I suppose we could strap a couple or Striking belts round 'er and
Drag her off"

"Are you #@&%ing mad!
"We'd end up causing a bleeding earthquake!"

Ted and I left the others to deliberate and
went back to the 2 vans outside;

"Lets take the dividing shelf out of our van and
Drop the two shells and Big Bertha across to theirs
That way we'll have a completely empty van and
More than enough space to take the mattress and its *occupant*"

"Capital Idea" said Ted

When we arrived back the census of opinion was that
We'd position three of us either side of the bed,
And lift the mattress to the floor;

Surprisingly, the idea actually *worked* and we had now accomplished
Phase **1** of
Operation Avoid Hernia;

We then covered the body up with a couple of sheets and
Somewhat unceremoniously
Trussed her up inside like a huge oven-ready chicken

To ensure that the dearly departed remained
on her new 'flying carpet'
We also slid two striking ropes under the
bed and secured them around
It and her for good measure;

"You'd better make sure no-one's around"
I said

"This is going to look pretty damn weird enough as it is without
Half of Abbey Wood looking on!"

With the striking belts firmly attached
We took the strain and, like a highly trained Tug-of-war team
Heaved, puffed, panted and rested our way
across the room to the door

"We're going to have to move her *onto her side* or we'll
Never get her through the door" said Ted.

"Sod that!" I thought
(But Ted was right, of course)

With a Samson-like effort
We heaved the mattress and contents over to one side

Four of us behind pushing for all it was worth
And two more at the back pulling the belts

With one last heave and a Richter registering thud, we **finally**
Got her out and into the hall!

"Just one problem"
Said Ted once more…

"There's no way we're gonna get *this lot* through the **FRONT** door!"

A quick check with the measuring tape and
Sure enough, door versus bed & corpse was a **no-win situation!**

Enter the carpenter …

*"I don't normally get calls to **REMOVE** a door"*
Said the man from the council

"I'm more use to *repairing* them after they've been
Kicked in!"

After explaining the urgency of the situation
(And appeasing the by now slightly curious husband)
Our 'newest 'team member' got to work on the front door and
Slowly but surely
Door and surrounding frame began to be removed;

At ***this*** point…

The police arrived!

It seems that
In our efforts to secure the 'cargo'

(Plus the fresh attempts to remove the offending front door)
We had, to use the vernacular
Been making enough noise

To wake the dead

(Personally; I think this would have been **quite useful** at the time
And would have saved a hell of a lot of hard
work! But it wasn't to happen)

Thanks to this and we were drawing
A fair amount of unwelcome attention and
I was beginning to regret the evening all the more

Luckily for us, the police saw the funny side of it

(Well, THEY would!
They weren't the ones who had damned near ruptured themselves
Trying to drag a 40+ stone women (with
Mattress Accessory) down the hallway!)

And helped cordon the area off and clear the vicinity of prying eyes
In readiness for our final…

'PUSH FOR FREEDOM'

Following a few 'last minute checks' we were finally…

All set

The door and frame were now sitting in the street and
The police were outside making bets as to which one of us
Would do his back in first!

THE LAST PHASE…

With Mattress and attached corpse finally in the gutter

All that was now left was to slide her into the van
(And count the hard-earned overtime!)

With one last gargantuan, gut busting, momentous *heave*
Six exhausted but very relieved undertakers
Were gasping their *victory breaths*

"*Thanks guys*"

I said

"We couldn't have done it without you"

The other's set off back to the yard leaving us to say our farewells to
The police, a much relieved husband and a
Now rather cheesed off council repairman who was
Trying to refit the frame and door he'd removed
only a few minutes beforehand

The Van strained under the weight as we waddled along
Woolwich road and back to the yard

"*Thank God **that's** over!*"
Said Ted

"Yeah, I know what you mean" I replied
"I've had more exercise tonight than I'd normally get in a **month**!"

As we pulled into the depot Ted leaned over and whispered…

"'*Ere, I've just another thought…*"

"Who's going to help us get her **OFF** the van?"

Me at 'Eltham Crem' - circa 1976

Train Spotting

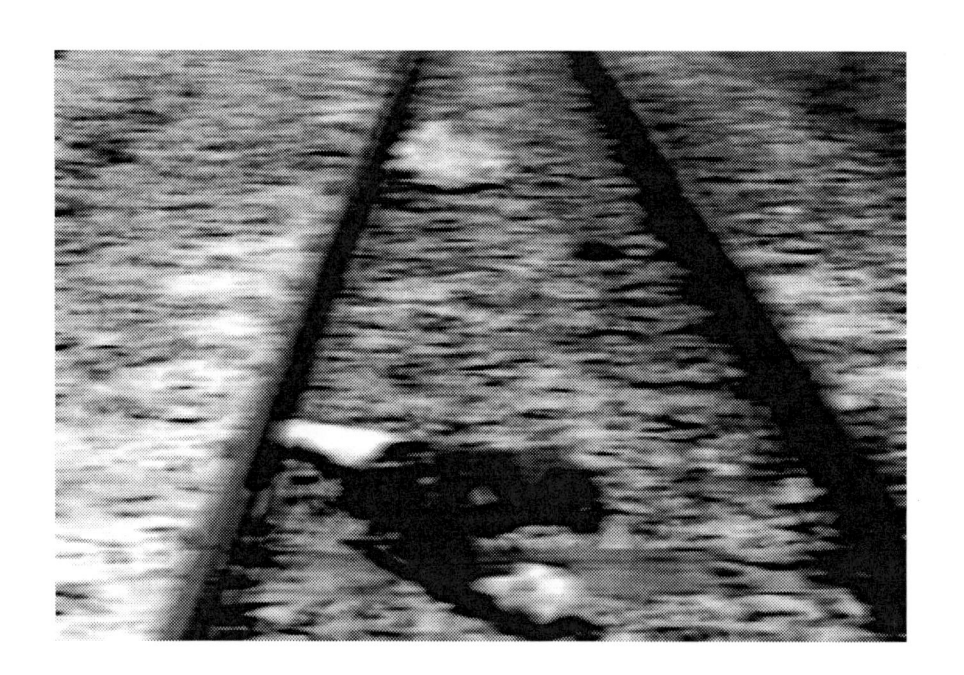

It had just gone nine in the evening when the phone rang…

"Get yourselves down to Erith Station and meet the boys
And police down there will you."

"Someone was hit by a train there a little while ago
And <u>what's left of him</u> need *collecting*!"

"I'd take a few extra carrier bags along too if I were you!"

According to the police, the young chap had been
seen walking along the platform at Erith and heading
off up the track towards Slade-Green.

As to whether he was just trying to get away without
Buying a ticket or there was something else involved'

I had no idea

Whatever the case, he'd met the 7.15 from Canon Street head on
And the train had come out **the winner!**

"We're got a few officers further down the track with torches
And the Rail people have just arrived to put up some
Proper lighting and turn off the power.

Keep to the side of the track until we give you the all clear.

About 200 yards up the track we could see torch lights
And so we headed off in that direction.

The low buzz of the live-rail stopped
As we got about half way there.

"Jesus, there's his bleedin' head over there!"
Said Graham with a mixture of shock and excitement.

"Excellent!"
Shouted the coroner

"We've been looking for that for some time!"

The empty train stood half a mile further down the track.
Shocked passengers and driver disembarked
And ferried off to Slade-Green some time earlier.

"We think we've found most of him"
Exclaimed the coroner

"Just look for the chalk marks or speak to the guys with torches
And they'll tell you where to look."

"Keep your eyes peeled and collect as much of him as you can;
I'll check what you've got when you're ready but don't expect to find
everything; there's a lot of foxes around here looking for **a free lunch!**"

For the next hour or so the three of us marched
Up and down the tracks in both directions
Looking for anything 'remotely human' to put in the carrier bags.

"I found one of his legs!"
Shouted Graham, jumping up and down like a demented school kid.

"It's not a #@&% competition for Christ sakes!"
I said
"Just get on with it will you; it's bloody cold out here".

Ted had gone to try and move the van as close
To the track as he could
(Luckily for us, Slade-Green Station was also
a cleaning and maintenance depot
So there was a siding pretty close by).

"A couple of the police-officers are bringing
the shell up from the depot"
He said

"The coroner wants us to drop all the bits in so that he can see
If we've got all of him or not"

Strangely enough, seeing bits of body, brain,
railway and alike all mixed up
Like a bloody cocktail in a coffin was bad enough but viewing it all
By torchlight somehow just made the whole thing
That much more;

Surreal

"Yeah, I reckon that's pretty much it!
You've got all the 'major parts'

I'll get the lads to do one more quick check but, otherwise
You can drop this lot back at the court in due course."

Just then the police arrived with some film
Taken from the station camera

"Excellent; let's see if we can put some kinda sense into all this"
Said the coroner.

"Never mind all that"
Shouted the man from the railway company
(Who had been pacing up and down uneasily
all the time we'd been standing there)

"I've got a <u>SERVICE</u> to run!

Can I tell 'em to turn the juice back on again?"

As we made our way back to the van we
could hear people on the platform
Moaning about the appalling service and the constant delays…

"This never used to happen in my days.
The trains always arrived on time back then"

Gone Swimming

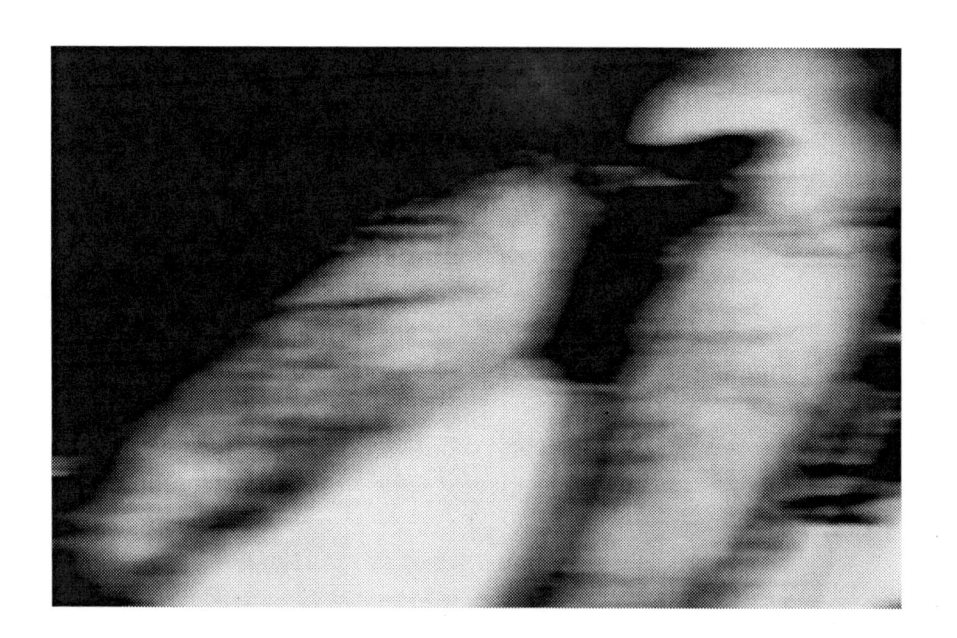

"Here, come and 'ave a look'"
Whispered Eric

"You've not seen a **floater** before have you?"

"No" I said
"I'm not sure I really want to!"

The river police just fished 'im out a couple of hours ago.
Come and see 'im while 'es still
FRESH"

Walking towards the mortuary you could already discern the awful smell

It was **like rotting fish** only **ten times worse!**

The stench got stronger and stronger the closer we got and it was
Almost overpowering at times;

"They reckon he fell in a few days back;
Judging by the skin colour and amount of bloating"

We arrived in the mortuary and, there, in front of me was
The most grotesque and disgusting sight I had ever encountered

It was like something out of an *old B-Movie*
But along with the twisted, inhuman shape came the
SMELL TO END **ALL SMELLS!**

Looking back I really don't know I managed to
Stop myself from throwing up at the time

The body was huge and bloated
The skin was grey and had an almost translucent quality about it

It was covered in patches of 'bluey green;
Blotches' like eccentric bruises and

Every now and then
Small *red patches* caught the eye

You could see 'tear marks' and gaping holes along the whole torso

Blackened veins mottled the whole of the body
Making it look like some kind of monstrous road-map!

The face was distended and grossly disproportioned
The left eye had been torn out and the other
Was blooded and oozing fluid

It looked more like some kind of deep sea creature than a human being

"They found him washed up near the Tate & Lyle docks"
Said Eric

"As far as we know, he went missing during a
Fishing trip in Dartford a few days back"

Just then the mortuary attendant arrived;

"Eric, you've got to speak to this poor chap's wife…
She's *insisting* on **viewing** the body!"

There's very little I can do to him to make him look; *presentable*"

"Here we go again" said Eric, "There's always one!"

I took a final look at the body;

"I hope to God he can be talk her out of it!"
I thought

It's in the Bag

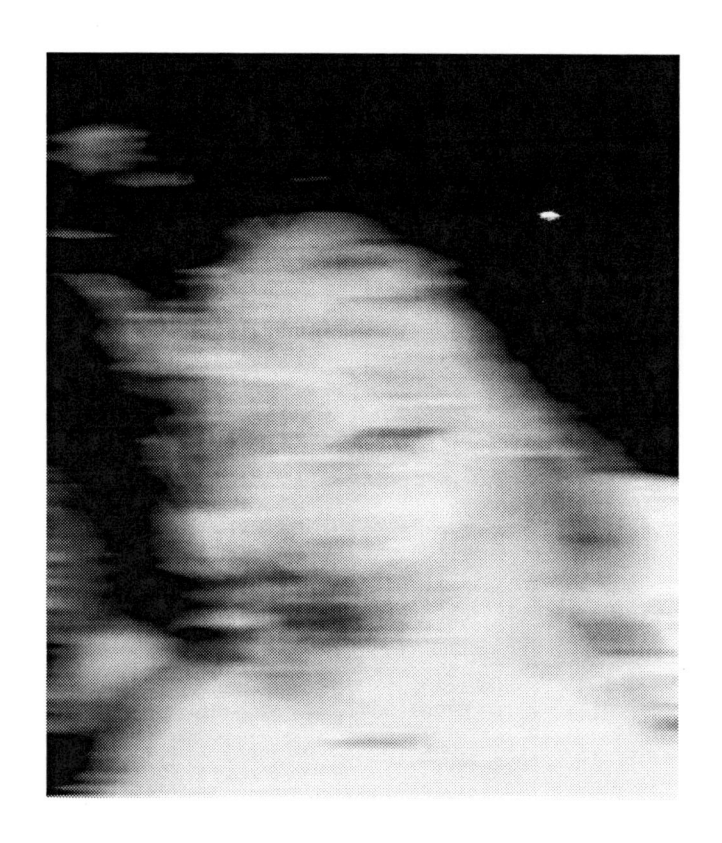

"Hey, this one's just up the road
To the Coroner's court"
Said Ted
"Excellent! *That'll save a lot of time".*

We arrived in a typical Greenwich road
Full of typical Greenwich houses

"No.16"… just by the coppers car

The policeman opened the door…
"You're going to *LOVE* this one"
He said
With 'one of *those smiles*' on his face

In the upstairs room
Lay the body of a young long haired man;
Naked from the waist down

On the bed beside him were numerous 'girly magazines' and a
Large bottle of Nivea Body Lotion

His right hand was resting on his *groin*!

Over his head
Was a transparent, plastic bag
Which draped downwards and
Was 'secured' by an elastic band wrapped
Tightly around his neck

"Coroner reckons he was playing the pink oboe (masturbating) and
Stuck the bag on his head for
'Added excitement!"

"Looks like the excitement got a little too much for him as
He popped his clogs as well as his load!"

"If *that's* **added excitement**

Said Ted
Staring bemusedly at the unfortunate young man

I'll think I'll stay...
CELIBATE!"

Ted then lowered his gaze;

"Erm, What are you going to do with *the magazines?*"
He said in an optimistic voice

"We're taking them back to the station for...

EVIDENCE"
Replied the policeman

"Yeah... **RIGHT!**" I said

"I always knew you copper's were a
Bunch of W***KERS!

Thank you for not Smoking

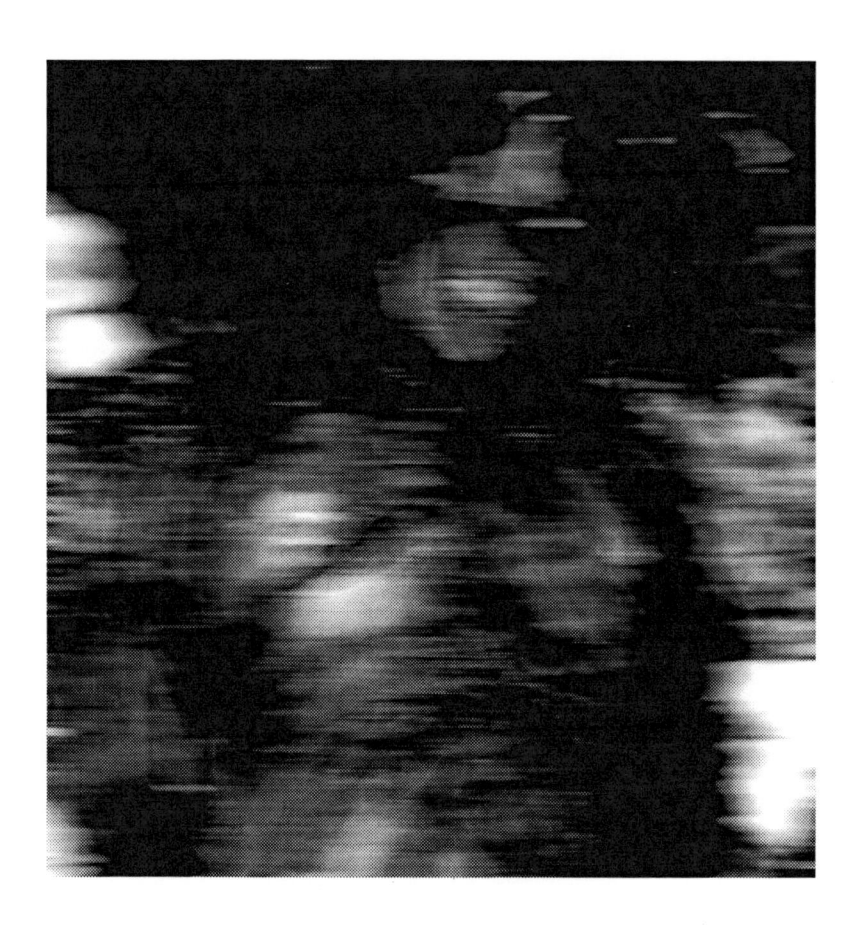

I REALLY hated these *types* of call!

I'd just got home and was sitting down
To mums special
Minced beef and baked-bean surprise
(The surprise being that it actually tasted a lot better than it sounded!)
And the bloody phone rang…

"Jesus Christ, I've only just got in!"

"Sorry… *death waits for nobody!*"
Said Ted
"You'll have to bung your dinner in the oven;
We've got a **burner** in Peckham."

I wasn't hungry *anyway!*

After picking up Graham on the way to Woolwich
We met Ted at the yard with the job details.

"The fire-brigade are still there and they've
Found one *crispy-fried corpse* in the bedroom;

I've got the gloves and air-freshener ready!"

We could see the blue lights flashing in the distance
And drove towards them

"We're here to collect the burner"
Said Ted to the one of the attending fire-crew
Without the slightest inkling of just how disrespectful it sounded

"Third house on the left;
Best see the fire-chief first as the stairs are'

A BIT DODGY!"

We pulled over and double-parked outside the house;

"Is the boss around?"
I said to the fireman rolling up the hose in the front garden

"Yeah, he's with the coroner
Go round the back and through white gate."

The coroner waved at us through the side-window
And we went through the back door and into the kitchen

He was standing there talking to the fire-chief;

"It's an upstairs fire"
He said

"Best let this chap lead the way *just in case*"

We followed the fire-chief through the kitchen door
And along a cramped corridor
There was a thick layer of black ash covering
the well-worn carpet which
'Crunched' like dry twigs as we walked along it

"**Most** *of the damage was confined to the main-bedroom*"

He said

"But you'd best be *careful* as we go up the stairs
As the fire caught hold of the stair-carpet and hand-rail too;

Still…I *THINK* it should be OK!"
(A comment that filled me with confidence at the time!)

Luckily, the body was in a room just
At the top right of the stairs

What was left of the door was sitting in splinters on
The floor and we could see scorch patterns and blistered paint
All around

Through the splinted doorway we could
See the charred and distorted body
Lying in the corner of the room, just in front of
A burnt out wardrobe;

Even though it was coated in a
Pelt of charred skin and melted clothing
We could just make out that it was the body of a
Young women
(Though it took some a degree of *imagination* to be sure)

"Another 'last cigarette' jobby!"
Said the fire-chief

"They really **ARE** bad for your health!"

I carefully trod across the waterlogged floor and
Gingerly leaned towards the misshapen body
Before tying the body label on to one of her blackened toes which
Somehow reminded me of the last sausage at
Harold's Summer Barbeque!

"She was only 24!"
Said Ted looking at the job-sheet

"What a stupid waste of life for the sake of
A quick fag before bedtime!"

By now, the smell of burning flesh was
Sticking to the air (and the back of my throat!)
And I was in no mood for hanging around

"Go get the stretcher will you;
I'm not taking a chance trying to
Bring a shell up these stairs!"

Graham and Ted carefully made their way down
The soggy stairs and back out to the van;

"Anyone else in the house when it happened?"
I asked

"Yeah, her father was downstairs when it started but
He didn't spot anything until it was well ablaze
He damned near choked to death himself and the
Ambulance crew didn't look too optimistic
when they carted him away
Either to be perfectly honest!"

I could hear Graham and Ted coming up the stairs

"Did you bring the gloves?"
I shouted

"Nah, I forgot. Do you want me to go back and get 'em?"

"No, leave it. We'll wash our hands in
The kitchen once she's bagged up."

As I grabbed her wrists, little flakes of burnt clothing
Dropped to the floor like black confetti and the
Oozing skin slipped crept and slid like wet soap
Forcing me to adjust and tighten my grip a few times
Before I finally managed to left her off the floor

"Jesus, it's like lifting a leper!"
I said and Ted nodded in sick agreement

We dropped her into the waiting
Stretcher and zipped it up.

"Where are you taking her?"
Said the fireman

"Greenwich Coroners Court"
I said

"They want her in the freezer ready for Monday"

How Ironic
I thought

Burnt to death one minute
Frozen solid the next!

There wasn't enough room for
All three of us
To walk down the stairs **together** and so
Being that I was the 'designated driver' for the evening
I designated **THEM**
To carry the stretcher back down the stairs!

The acrid smoke was stifling
Making our eye's run and the short journey down the stairs
Seem like hiking up Mount Everest

The front door was blocked with
Debris and furniture removed from upstairs and so
We were forced to manoeuvred the stretcher round the
Bottom of the stairs and out through the
Kitchen and then finally through the little
Garden to the waiting van outside

We closed the van doors and
Returned to wash our hands'

"The water's off!"
Said one of the fireman
"You'll have to wash your hands somewhere else"

"Typical!" I thought
"Bloody gallons of the stuff all over the house but
Not a single drop for **us**!"

We jumped back in the van and headed off for Greenwich

"OK then…"

Said Ted

Who's for a *KEBAB!*"

RTA (Road Traffic Accident)

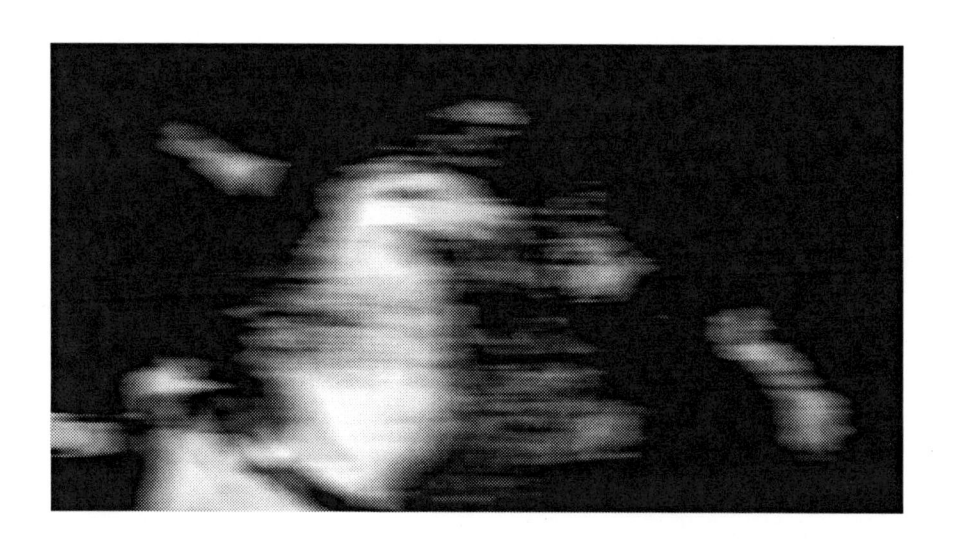

We were just about to leave The Brook Hospital, Woolwich
And head off back to the yard when the pager went off

"Great, **MORE** bloody work!" I said

After disappearing to ring the office
Brian came back to the van

"We've got an RTA in Charlton" he said

"Can't the ambulance crew
Drop 'im off at the hospital?"

"Nah… apparently they're off to another job so
The police are hanging on for us to go and collect it"

Charlton was just up the road and
Luckily we still had an empty shell on the van

"It should be just off the High Street"
Said Ted with his usual degree of *map-reading optimism.*

Of course, as expected, we went up and down a few
'Likely roads' before **finally** arriving
At the RIGHT one

The police car was down one the end of the road
And access was blocked off with yellow police tape
Just beside the police car we could make out
A white sheet covered in crimson stains

"It's a REAL mess this one!
Half 'is guts hanging out and bones
Sticking out everywhere!
Hit and run too"
Shouted the Copper with no
Obvious concern as to who else heard

HE WASN'T JOKING!

I don't know **WHAT** it was that had hit this poor sod
But, whatever it was,
It must have been BIG and going like a Bat out of Hell as
His body was literally *flattened* in several places and
Bent and twisted in ways
No human body was ever designed to be

Both his legs were at *right-angles* to his hips and
One of his wrists was snapped and
Dangling down from his arm

Just under his left armpit, his rib-cage had been
Smashed open and an
Assemblage of entrails and
Assorted innards were hanging out
Like a huge plate of Linguini

Despite 'the mess' it was *just* about possible
To derive that we were looking at the body of a *young* chap
Late teens or thereabouts

He was wearing a dark green jacket and
tracksuit bottoms both of which
Were torn in several places and coated in blood and guts

"Get the mop and bucket"
I said to Ted

"Can't the police do that?"

"Yes, they *COULD* but we might as well do it
At the same time as we remove the body or
Do you think we should just leave *half his guts*
In the middle of the road for the next half hour?"

Ted wasn't squeamish…

He was just…

LAZY!

We slid the stretcher down beside the body;

"Careful!"
"You nearly shoved the stretcher into his lower intestines!"
Said Ted

"I don't want to have to clean the van and
The stretcher *too* when we get back!"

Make that…

REAL Lazy!

It was a real job getting hold of him properly
to place him in the stretcher

Every time I tried grabbing an arm or a leg
It started to bend with a sickening crack
That sent shivers down my spine

"Get *the **board*** will ya! We'll have to slip it under
Him to lift him off the ground"

"**YOU** can bend down beside him"
Ted replied
"I'm not kneeling in a pile of guts for anyone!"

(Sometimes Ted's compassion was… *OVERWHELMING!)*

We placed the long wooden board
That we kept in the van for such occasions
Beside him and slowly manhandled his
mangled body over and on to it

It was then a relatively simply matter to
Move the board off the ground and onto the stretcher

"The bloody zip won't do up with the board inside"

Said Ted in his normal
'Now that it's too late… here are some words of wisdom' manner'

"Well…
Drape the sheet over it and drape it underneath.
We've only got to
Make it a few feet to the back of the van."

The white sheet
Now soaked with blood and dirt
Was tucked in to the stretcher for the short trek

"Don't worry Ted" I said
We'll throw the sheet away when we get back to the yard;
You **WONT** have to clean it!"

"Forget that…" he said
I could do with a new sheet!"

(I *HOPED* he was only joking
But, knowing Ted …)

We slid the stretcher into the van and then
With mop and bucket in hand
Returned to the clean away the remaining mess from the road

"Wow, you lot think of everything huh!"
Said the policeman who was now removing the yellow police tape
"I thought the council cleaned this sort of thing up?"

"Yeah, they normally do but we carry some
Disinfectant and alike for those 'messy moments' and
It's no skin off my nose to finish the job properly."

"When you're finished…
Can you pop round **my** house and
Give that the once over too!" he smiled

"No worries!" I said…

"I'll send **TED** over to do it!"

ON YOUR BIKE!

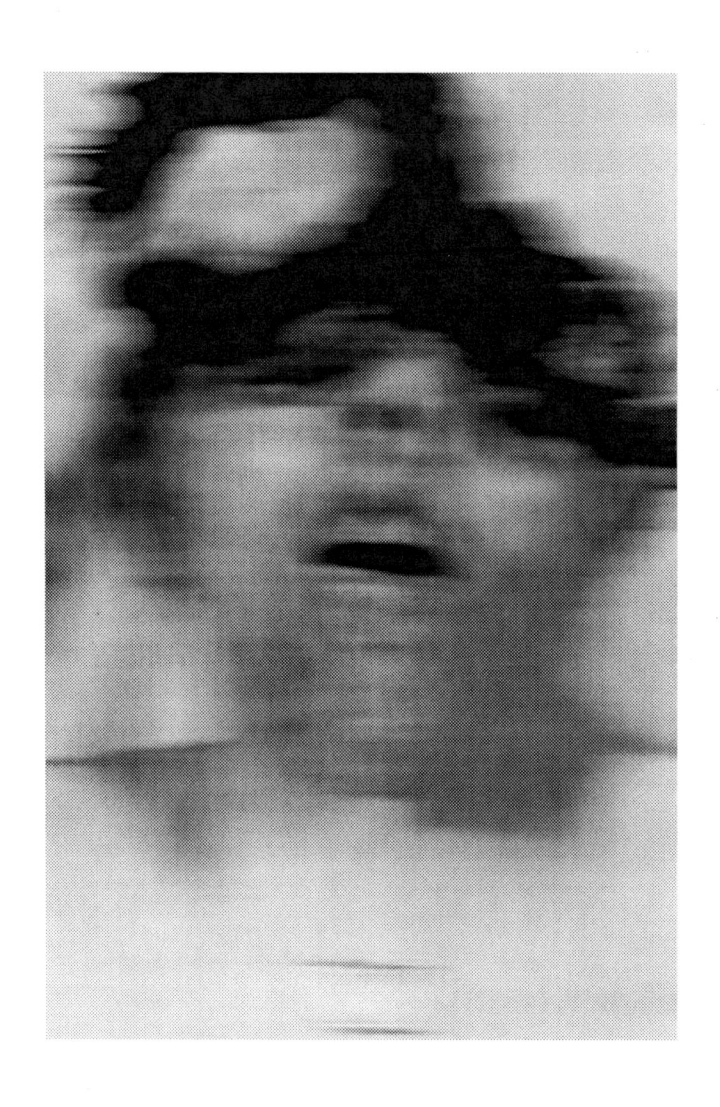

There are laws in this country of ours
And most; if not **all**; should be *obeyed*

One law I will most **definitely** adhere to myself
Is the one that states that you…
MUST wear a crash helmet when riding a motorcycle

When the call came in to collect an RTA
From down by the Woolwich Ferry roundabout
I thought *our luck was in* …

"Forget the van lads;
We can bloody ***walk*** this one!"

The police had blocked the roundabout off and, in the distance
We could see an articulated lorry
Half on road; half on the roundabout itself

As we got closer, we could make out the
mangled remains of a motorcycle
Wrapped around one of the massive rear wheels of the lorry

"Where's the rider?"
I said to the policeman directing traffic

"You'll find **most** of him underneath the front of the lorry!"
He said

"The firemen are trying to retrieve the *last bit*
From the wheel arch as we speak."

We parked the van behind the lorry and
I crawled between the two and towards the body which
Had just been pulled out from underneath

The fire crew place a red-blanket over the body
That had been *donated* by the ambulance crew
Who had left just before we arrived

Pulling the blanket back a little to see
Which end was which
(It wouldn't do to tie the body label on the 'wrong end'!)
I gasped in surprise at the sight that greeted me underneath

"Where the f* is the TOP OF HIS HEAD???"**
I blurted out aloud

Looking towards the front of the lorry
I suddenly realised
My earlier question had now been *answered...*

Apparently, the rider hadn't braked in time and
Had gone straight across the roundabout and
Into the side of the lorry

He had been out 'joyriding' with some mates on
His 'borrowed' motorbike but hadn't had
The sense to *borrow the*
CRASH HELMET!

Eye-witnesses said that he'd
Hit the side of the container head on (literally!)
And with such force that it had
Sliced the top half of his skull off
Like a 3 minute egg!

At the point of impact
The top part of his head had
Departed company with the rest of his face and had ended up
Squashed between one of the huge rear wheels of the lorry

Looking even closer I could see that
One of his eyes was splattered up the side of the lorry
And the other one could be seen dangling
Inside what was left of his head!

Bits of disintegrated brain were also coating the tyres and
Most sickening of all…

His left ear was firmly wedged
In a metal strut under the container

I lifted up the remaining piece of his skull
Which had been 'flipped over' and peeled back like an orange and
Now lay tucked *behind* the back of his forehead and
Gently pulled it up and tried to slot it back into place
However it had been *compressed* and shattered by the impact and
Wouldn't fit despite my best efforts

Staring down I could see that there was still a large tuft of
Jet black hair sticking out from the top and
I could even make out the signs of *a parting!*

Ted came back with a carrier-bag containing whatever bits he and
The Fire Brigade had managed to find

"Most of the brain's been washed away by the
Fire hoses along with several pints of blood"

*"I wouldn't light a fag up either if I were you Ted;
It reeks of petrol round here too!"*
I said

Ted surveyed the state of the mangled body;

"I think we've got some sticky tape in the van;
Do you want me to get it and try and stick
this **big bit** back on again?"

"No, I don't think my stomach could take it!
Just stick it in a bag and shove it in the shell with him for now"

I wrapped the blanket back round and we
lifted the body up and into the shell

"Mind how you go!"
Said Ted
You nearly bumped his **HEAD**!"

"Yeah… Right…VERY funny!"

"Guys, Guys… I found an earring"
Shouted Graham

"Just the ONE?"

"Yep!"

"OK. Stick it in the bag with the ear
If it turns out **not** to be his…
You can claim it for your own in a few weeks time!"

"The ear or the earring?" Smirked Graham

"Is everyone a bloody comedian round here!"

"I think I'll pass anyway' said Graham
With a look of disgust on his face

As we walked back towards the van we could see the Lorry Driver
Still sitting in the police-car
Holding a cigarette in his shaking hand

"I **couldn't** stop!
He just came straight at me!"
He said

"I wouldn't worry mate"
"Even with a crash helmet on
It probably wouldn't have made any difference anyway;

*You can't blame yourself for **someone else's stupidity**"*

The lorry driver glanced at us through vacant as we walked by
His face as grey as dust and his head bowed low

"It's **HIM** I feel sorry for"

Said Ted

"Probably haunt him for the rest of his life this will"

"Yeah
It's always the **innocent** that suffer"

"This is one funeral I hope <u>I</u> don't end up on"
I said

"Right…
Shall we head off back to the yard then?"
Said Graham

"<u>HEAD</u> OFF!!!"
Said Ted
With that *totally inappropriate* grin of his

"<u>**I'M**</u> the one who
Tells the jokes around here!"

SPLITTING IMAGE

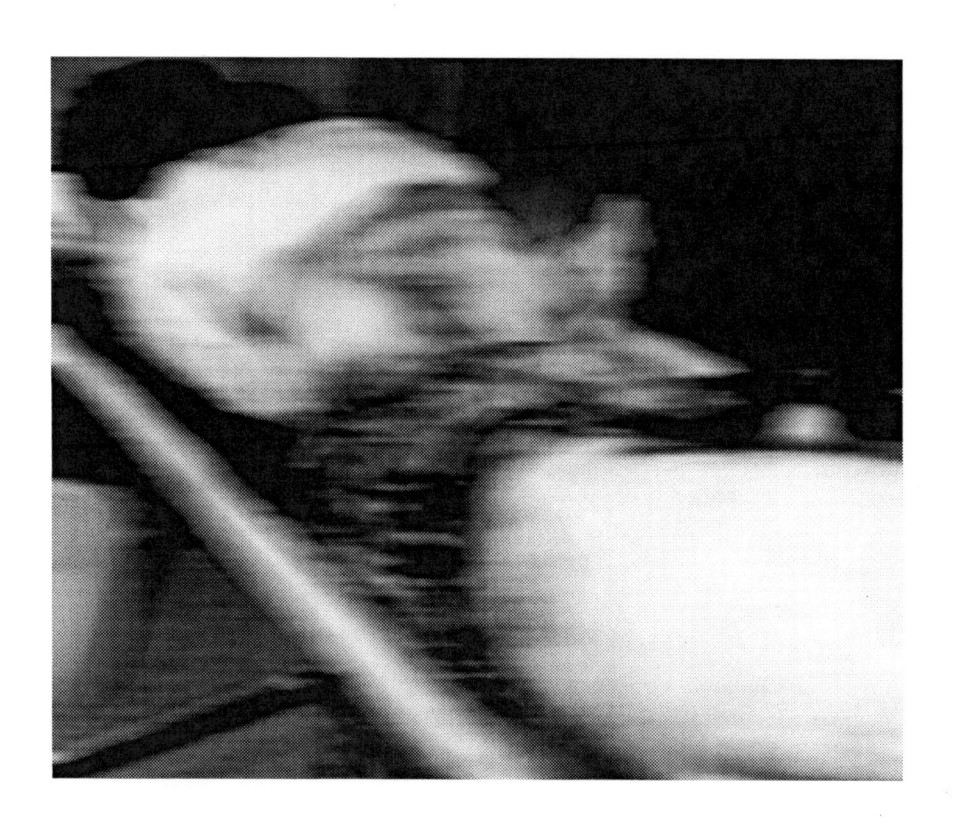

It had been a bad month for *people* **but…**
A **good** month for ***UNDERTAKERS!***

The cold snap had killed off many of the
Old folks who, thanks more than ever to
Government cutbacks and alike
Were dropping like flies of hypothermia

The recession too was taking its toll and
We'd had more than our fair share of suicides too

YEP…
All in all…

Things were shaping up
VERY NICELY INDEED!

As I was daydreaming about all the extra overtime I was soon to get…
Ted walked in with some more…
GOOD NEWS

"We've got another *jumper*" he said

"Excellent!"
I replied
"What a great week this is turning out to be!"

We were told that a white male had jumped from a block of flats
Just off the A2

When we got there the ambulance was just leaving and
The police were waving at us from the edge of the estate

"Typical…
Right across a muddy field!"
"So much for that *'great week'*"
I thought

I left Ted to park the van up and Graham and I
Walked over to where the police were standing;

"You might want to tell your driver to park round the *other* side"
One of them said

"You can probably lift *this bit* over the fence to him from here then"

This **BIT**?
I thought and
Then it dawned on me…

On our side of the fence
We could only see the **TOP** *half* of the body!

"It was dire enough jumping from *up there* in the **first** place"
Continued the policeman
Pointing in the general direction of the adjacent flats

"But… Talk about **bad luck…**"

*Managing to land on the only **fence** for miles!"*

Looking over to the somewhat battered wooden fence
Now topped with entrails and coated in blood we could see that it had

SLICED HIM IN TWO!

Now… the **top** half of his torso lay half buried in the
Muddy grass **THIS** side of the fence and

The remaining half was lying on the other side hidden from our view!

Ted arrived and looked at us from the other side of the fence…

"Er, you guys. You ain't gonna believe that but…

THERE'S **ANOTHER** BODY THIS SIDE TOO!"

"Yeah…
Nice try Ted but…
That bit actually belongs to **THIS** bit over here!"

"Oh" he said
"I thought it was a tad strange;
I mean;
You don't normally get **two** of 'em jump
At the same time do you!"

"And… you worked that all out by
Yourself did you Ted?"
I said in my best sarcastic voice

Ted just *ignored me…*

*"Since all I can see is two legs sticking up in the air
I take it you've got the top half over there then?"*

I wish now that we could have seen it from *Ted's side* as
It sounded a **whole** lot *funnier* than what we could see

(I suppose you could say that it was only…
HALF *as funny!)*

"What do you want me to do?
Get a stretcher or what?"

"Nah, we'll pass our bit over to you then you wait there and
We'll walk round and bring the shell to you"

We bundled 'our half up' and passed it to Ted over the fence;

"You can start getting the guts off of the fence and
Into the carrier-bags too whilst you're waiting"

"#@%£ing charming!

I get all the *plum* jobs!"

It only took a few minutes to trudge across
the field and around to Ted

"Bloody guts!
I hate them!" he said

"Ah quit your moaning and bung the bag in the shell will ya!"

We unceremoniously placed the two pieces of body
In to the shell and closed the lid;

"I hope you've got 'em the *right way round*"
Said Graham

"We wouldn't want you to stick his head up his ar*e would we!"

"I'll stick his head up **YOUR** ar*e if you don't stop Mucking about!
Now… Did someone remember to put the body label on?"

"I stuck **TWO** on"
Said Ted with that all too familiar grin on his face

"I shoved one on his big toe and another on his …
(Grin widens!)

FINGER!"

Just in case he gets
Separated!"

"Yeah…
REAL clever Ted!" I replied

How many *half-people* have we picked up this week then?"

"I think;
Even *without* the body label(s)
We'd have worked that one out, don't you?"

"Yeah, he's wearing a tracksuit with **matching** top and bottoms!"
Said Graham
Adding his two penneth

"Sometimes…
I despair with you two
I **really** do!"

We scurried back to the van
No doubt watched by hundreds of morbid eyes

All the time
We could see
Little windows;
In little flats;
With little people;
Staring

It always made me laugh when
People hid behind curtains
The moment you looked in their direction
As if they were doing something
Naughty or were terrified of being

Caught out"

"One good thing with hi-rise flats…
You get a good view of all the misery 'out there'"
said Ted

"Yep;
Life can be a *funny old game* at times"
I replied

"It's a game of **TWO HALVES**"
Retorted Graham

It wasn't *really* appropriate'

But we laughed **anyway**!

For Better or For Worse

The Social Workers were still trying to get
The old girl out of the house
When we arrived

The police were there too but seemed
Reluctant to *'get involved'*

In the end, it was the Public Health Inspector
Who ordered her out of her *own* house and so
She was finally but;
VERY GENTLY
Escorted out through the front door and
Into the waiting police-car

We'd already 'been warned' and had
Started to get into the 'ET Suits'
As soon as we were given the nod

I always hated wearing the *ET Suit*
It was bad enough having to wear a suit & tie anyway but to
Then have to squeeze
In to a sealed up plastic boiler-suit
Was quite frankly
A real pain in the #@$%!

"He's in the main bedroom
Up the stairs; first door on the left"
Said the coroner

We 'heavy breathed' our way into the house and
Climbed the narrow stairs to the top

The staircase was filthy and the stair carpet had seen
Better days

Even 'through the suits' we could smell the
Rancid stench of death which became
More and more nauseating the closer we got
To the top of the stairs

As we neared the bedroom, we spotted
An old Zimmer-frame
Standing by the door
The last testament to an old mans life

Through the half opened door we spied an old metal bed and
Even from this distance, we could see that
The room was swarming with flies

As we moved closer, we also observed that the bed was
Alive with maggots

As we crossed the room
Fleas were bouncing off our suits trying for
One more free meal as we proceeded
Towards the bed

On the wall above the bed was a
Faded embroidered cloth in an aging frame

It read…

REST HERE WEARY TRAVELLER

The old fella (or what was left of him!)
Was sat bolt-upright in the bed

He was wearing blue and white striped pyjamas
Which were rancid and covered in *Jip*

There were gaping holes in his emancipated face
From which curious maggots were now peering and
Every now and then
I heard a tiny little 'plop'
Against my protective suit as fleas and flies
Relentlessly dive-bombed us
As we walked around the room

"I can't believe the old girl was **still** sleeping in *THIS* bed'
Said Ted

"She must have **completely** lost it.
It's enough to make you *vomit!*"

"I wouldn't advise it"
I said

"At least not until **AFTER** you take the ET suit off!"

From all accounts, the coroner reckoned
He'd been dead best part of a month

And, in all that time, she had continued on with
THEIR lives as if
Nothing had changed

"They reckon something just snapped in her head and
That she just couldn't accept the fact that he was dead"

On the table next to the bed sat one solitary card with the words;

HAPPY 50th ANNIVERSARY on it

"I reckon if you'd been married to someone
THAT LONG, the old fella probable **WAS**
Her life"
Said Ted

They think he had a heart attack and
Passed away peacefully in his sleep

Ever since then
She'd cooked him food and
Dutifully brought him cups of un-drunk tea
Before clearing away the untouched dishes

Day and Night she had continued to be
The loving, doting wife and had refused to
Let *death* interfere with her love for him

*"Why the hell it took social services so long
To discover the truth, God only knows!"*
I said

But they were old people and old people
Have a way of going;
Unnoticed

I found myself staring at the anniversary card and
Felt a rare tear run down my face

Over the years I'd become *hardened* and
Desensitised to death
It was the only sane response to an often insane situation
But there were times when the sorrow just
Got to you;

"I hope when I find someone special
She loves me half as much as this"
I said

"<u>HE</u> probably will"
Said Tony

Trying to inject a much need air of humour in to the moment

We placed the stretcher down beside the bed and
Swept aside the ravenous maggots before
Pulling back the sheets

Slowly we started to lift his frail body off of the bed;

"JESUS!"
Screamed Tony

"I'VE PULLED HIS #@&£ING FOOT OFF!"

Sure enough, Tony stood; half terrified
Half in shock; holding onto a moth-eaten sock
From which the old fella's foot could be seen
Dangling from the leg

"Christ, he's falling apart!
Drop him in the stretcher now before;
Anything else 'falls off!"

We unceremoniously dumped the
Pile of pyjama clad bones into the stretcher
With his foot hanging to the side
Held on by a few sinewy tendons

As I bent down to zip the stretcher up I could
see that his jaw had *dropped* and
Just for a moment, it looked as if he was actually;
Smiling!

"Maybe he knows ***she's*** waiting outside for him?"
Said Tony with a sadness not at all his own

We lifted the stretcher and slowly walked
back to the top of the staircase;
"Give me the stretcher" I said
"It'll be easier if I carry it down over my shoulder after all
There's nothing of him"

When we got to the front door
The public health team were 'suiting up' outside
Ready to fumigate the place

"It's all yours fella's" I said and
Headed in the direction of the van

'The old Girl' was still sitting in the police car
Motionless and vacant
Seemingly unaware of the whole world around her

Suddenly, she looked over towards us and
Wailed in pitiful sorrow

The sound cut through me like a knife and
I felt a lump in my throat as yet another tear run down my face

To us; he was long dead but
To her; she was just realising
For the very first time
That *her love* was gone

Forever

I knew nothing about her but
I could almost *taste* her sadness

"That's the trouble with love' remarked Tony
"The more you love someone;
The harder it is to let them go"

We loaded the stretcher onto the van and took off our E.T. Suits

"Thank god we're out of those things" said Tony
"It was like being in a sauna!"

2 months later;

We buried her alongside her husband

FRED

Fred had joined the Co-op about a year after me and had already gained a bit of a reputation as someone…
'Best avoided'

Not that there was anything nasty of vindictive about him (indeed, deep down, Fred was well known to be the sort of person who would put himself out for his fellow man and it was even rumoured that, beneath that haggard and rough persona of his, there beat a heart of gold) but it took a *'special kind of person'* to work with Fred.

The problem was that; whereas most undertakers had developed a natural etiquette and aptitude when it came to dealing with the public at their Most vulnerable and depressed, **Fred** had never quite managed the art of diplomacy and was, Quite frankly…
About as subtle as a ***flamethrower!***

In effect;

Fred was the undertaker equivalent of
A Square Peg in a Round hole!

(Indeed, the general census of opinion was that Fred was *either;*
Secretly related to someone 'high up' or that
The Personnel Officer had a sense of humour!)

Anyway, today was
Christmas Eve
And volunteers for the *skeleton crew*
(Yes, sorry, on reflection this wasn't really the
best pseudonym to have chosen!)
Were thin on the ground and so, for *today* at least,
It was me, Tony and **Fred**!

The day started off innocuously enough with the three of
us, plus assorted ancillary staff brewing up the morning
tea and making breakfast ready for the day ahead.

Fred; who was a bit of a chain smoker; was waffling on
about something or other in his best Louis Armstrong drawl
and stirring a cup of stewed tea when, *suddenly…*
He started convulsing and growling like a **demented werewolf!**

The chatter stopped and all eyes fell up
Fred as the *dull undulating sound*
And accompanying *facial spasms* **gripped us all…**
"I think 'es gonna have a #@%$ing heart attack!"
Whispered Tony

"Nah, he's nowhere blue enough in the face!
Maybe it's **just** *a stroke!"* informed the embalmer
(Who had a smattering of medical knowledge and therefore
Considered himself the latter say Doctor
McCoy (Bones?) of the Co-op

At this point, Fred looked as if he was chewing a hand grenade and
His eyes were starting to roll as he reached *deep* into his stomach

"Christ, he's going to **throw up!**"
Tony remarked which
Sent everyone leaping for cover and running in all directions

Seconds that seemed like eons passed when suddenly
The choking stopped and
With one last sickening heave
Fred finally coughed up a large 'lump' of something resembling
The rolling stone that gathered no moss!

"Err...Yuk" said Tony with people those few
still remaining agreeing in harmony

"That's #@£$ing gross!"

Now, most of us had seen many a sight that would have cleared
The odd stomach or two, but seeing Fred's
flemmy cat-furr-ball on a plate trick
Had several of us (including me I'm sorry to say)
Heading for the toilet

Suffices to say;
There was a lot of *un-eaten toast* that morning!

Fred carried on stirring his tea as if nothing had happened;

"I'm off to the van" I said

"Tell **Garfield** to meet us when he's finished
nauseating everyone, will you"

I hurried off to the van to check the job sheet

Being Christmas Eve all the hospital mortuaries were closed
so we just had a couple of 'house' jobs for the day before
we could all go home to enjoy the festive period.

Tony and our 'new crew member' arrived and Fred lit another
cigarette before coughing and wheezing his way into the cab.

"Are you sure you should be smoking those things?"
I said

"I'm pretty sure that;
Coughing up half a lung at the breakfast;
Isn't **good** for you!"

"Nah, it ***weren't*** a lung"
Fred replied in his best Neanderthal
"It was too ***hard*** for that!"

"**Hard!**
Said Tony with a look of nauseated horror

How the hell would you know that?"
All at once realising that this wasn't the sort of question
Either of us **really** wanted to know the answer to;

"*I tried **cutting it with me knife**!*"
Said Fred
Seemingly oblivious to just how gross his comment was

We drove out in silence;
Both of us with numb with revulsion and a strong desire
Never to speak to Fred again!

It had been snowing overnight and the whole world
(Well, at least *the bit* we could see)
Was covered in a glorious white frosting

*Even **Woolwich** look 'pleasantly picturesque' for a change!*

"Old fella; late 80's; just off the Old Kent Road"
Barked Ted reading the job sheet

Although the snow made a nice change
(As did the fact that the council had actually
gritted the main roads too!)
It made the side roads a hazardous
But we took our time and eased our way down
the narrow snow-covered side road
To the address we'd been given.

It was a big old house with several steep
steps leading up to the front door;
"You wait here with Fred and I'll go and check things out"
I told them
And climbed out of the smoke filled van

A young lady answered the door;

"Hello madam. We're from the Co-op"

"Yes; Come on in"
"We've been expecting you"

The house was old and musty with Spartan Christmas decorations
Hanging limply from the ceiling
At the end of the corridor sat a dilapidated Christmas tree
On a small wooden table with a few Christmas Cards on it

"Grandma is in *here*" She said
Beckoning to the door on the right

"She's still with *grandfather* but has made her
peace and knows **why** you're here"

I followed her in to the room to find an old grey haired
lady sitting in a big open chair next to a settee where
the old chap's body was lying, under a blanket;

"Grandma" she whispered gently
"The undertakers are here"
The old lady turned to look at me and smiled;

"Thank your Dear.
Sorry to bring you out on Christmas Eve"
She said

"Think nothing of it madam. We're very sorry for your loss"

Slowly the old lady stood up and was helped to another
chair near the window by her granddaughter;

"I'm just going to fetch my colleagues" I said
"Perhaps you and your grandmother would
prefer to wait in another room?"

"No thank you dear" said the old lady
"I'd like to be with him when he *goes*"

"Of course; that's your decision" I said
And made my way back to the front door to beckon Tony and Fred;
"Nice and careful chaps"
I said

"The widow and her granddaughter are in the room with him so
let's do it by the book and be on our best behaviour shall we"

We carefully manoeuvred the wooden shell along
the corridor and stood it on its foot so that we could
swivel it around and in through the door;

"Go and get the striking belt" I said to Tony
"We'll need it when we bring the coffin back out again"

I looked over to the two women;

"It's it OK if we *proceed* ladies?"

"Of course" the old lady replied and waved her hand in approval

I gently pulled the blanket back and discretely attached
The body label to the old chap's big toe;

"**Fred...** Would you take the gentleman's feet?" I said
"Now, together and on the count of 3…
1…2…3

We lifted the frail body and tenderly lowered it into the shell
Before placed the lid back on

Tony arrived back with the belt…

"Lift the coffin up please gentlemen"
"And I'll slide the belt underneath"

"So far, so good"
I thought to myself

But, it was at ***this stage*** that,
For reasons only **HE** will know…

Fred decided to engage the old lady in conversation…

"Been married long love?"

"Yes"
She said
"We celebrated our
Golden Anniversary
Last year"

"Gold. Wow!"
"That's a *bleeding long time!*

I've only been with my Doris 10 years and
*I already hate the sight of the **OLD BAT!**"*

"*'Erm, **Fred**…*" I said
But it was too late…

"Mind you, I suppose, when you're as old as you *two old buggers*
There 'Ain't a lot of point playing the field!

That said, I bet you were a **bit of a goer**
When you were young eh?"

"I wouldn't like to say"
Replied the old lady
Now looking rather flustered and taken aback

"It's not *the sort of thing that a lady* discusses
Especially not in front of her *grand-daughter!*"

"Sorry love;
Just trying to make you *feel better!*

Mind you; at your age…
I don't suppose it'll be much longer before you'll be
'Back beside him' anyway will it?"

"RIGHT GENTLEMEN!"
I said

"Shall we leave these good people to themselves and
Be on our way"

"Yeah, suppose so"
Mumbled Fred

"We can't stay 'ere talking all day

We've got another **couple of stiff's** to pick-up before
I can get back to Doris's Christmas Pud!"

Tony and I grabbed the coffin and
Made for the door as fast as
Our legs and decorum would allow;

"Nice meeting ya ladies"

Said Fred
Following on behind

"Hope you have a

NICE CHRISTMAS!"

THE REAL TERROR

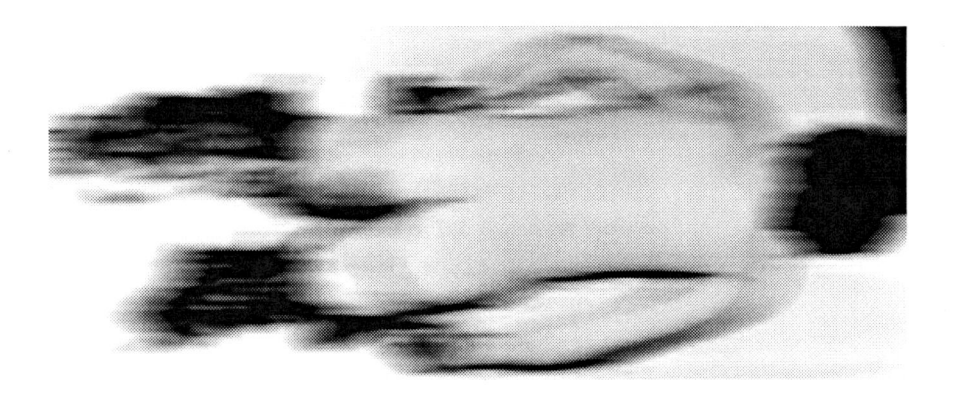

Background – Nowadays the world is a troubled place but this is nothing *new*. In the 70's/80's we had 'our own' problems in the UK and I shall never forget the day that we 'got a call' to attend the aftermath of a bomb attack in London. Our 'pick-up' was a middle-age family man who had simply been *in the wrong place at the wrong time* and had become another 'faceless victim' of the time.

At the time I was quite badly affected by the atrocity and carnage that confronted me and the images I saw that day will remain with me *forever*. I have to say that I also found it 'quite hard' to share my experiences too but, for some reason, I found the medium of *'poetry'* helped me express emotions that I had found difficult to put in to 'words' so here is the piece that I wrote at the time…

He was off to work as usual
He kissed his wife goodbye
Little did he realise
That it was his turn to die

The cowards who had laid the trap
Were watching their new *prey*
They knew he'd die when he walked by
But pressed the button *anyway*

A blinding flash; a plume of smoke
The bomb had done its job
He was just another faceless victim;
One more family left to sob

The force of the explosion
Tore through his flesh and bone
Shattering his body;
At home; **she** grabbed the phone

The tears poured down
The children wept
*Daddy was **never** coming back*
One more victim;
One more day;
*One more **terrorist attack***

Through Undertakers Eyes

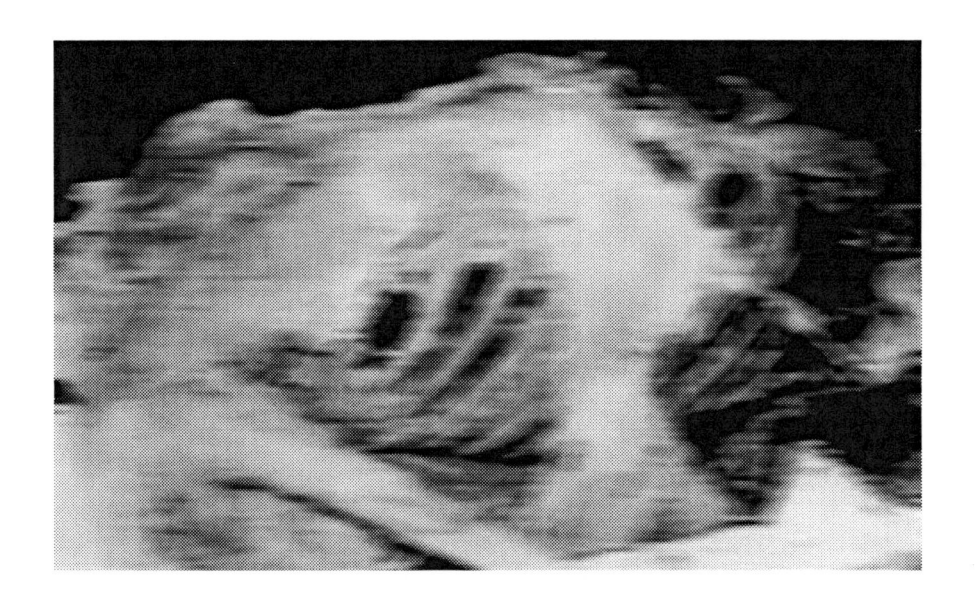

If you ever saw a dead body
Dragged from the sea
It's bloated, translucent skin
Blackened and mottled
Bones protruding
Through gaping
Pus ridden holes
Not even sure
What sex IT is
Not even sure
If *IT* was human

THEN

You'd know why
*I **STILL** have nightmares*

In all the years
That I worked as
An undertaker
I saw sights
No mortal man
Should have to see

Decapitated souls
Bodies mutilated

An encounter with a train making a
Mockery of flesh and bone

An old man
Who, once dead
Became his little dogs dinner
Along with the maggots
That feasted on him

We once called
Upon an old man
Who was found
Lying in his bed
Half decomposed
Still in his pyjamas
With his doting widow still sharing it
Night after night
Not willing or able to grasp the
Reality of his death

He was so badly decomposed that
His foot *came loose* when we tried to lift him up
A faint unearthly cry
As the last vestige of breath was
Squeezed from his
Long dead lungs

The body of a HUGE woman
Whose individual thigh
Was larger than my *waist!*
Her adoring husband
Telling us that
She used to eat a
Family sized tub of ice cream a day
As a SNACK!

Trying to explain to him
Why we had to wait
For *more men* to arrive
Because of her
Immense proportions

Unable to lift her
We had to take
The stained bed

That was her home
With us

The van
Creaking and groaning
Under the strain of
Such weight

I suppose
*Worst of **all** were;*

THE **CHILDREN**

Born to extinction

Traumatized and inconsolable
Parents looking at ME
Taking their beloved child away
As if I was
The Devil incarnate

This was the one time
Being hard was…

HARD

In the end and out of sight
I end up lending my tears
To theirs
In genuine; unavoidable
Sympathy

I saw death
In every sickening facet
Living the nightmare every day of my life and the
At **night**;

Vivid images and recollections of those
Sights unimaginable
Haunting every dream

I will NEVER be the same person again
How could I be?

For I've seen life…

THROUGH UNDERTAKERS EYES

CURRENT & FORTHCOMING PUBLICATIONS

An Undertaker's Diary is Paul's 3rd book (details of books 1 & 2 can be found on the next page) and he is now working on book number 4 (which is effectively the sequel/sister book to this one).

Whilst An Undertaker's Diary dealt with the darker, more gruesome elements of Paul's life as an undertaker, his next publication (tentatively entitled; 'IT'S YOUR FUNERAL') focus on the more 'formal duties' (namely the funerals themselves).

Having attended and carried out literally hundreds of funerals (when not 'collecting' the contents of the coffins that is!) Paul's next book tells the 'stories' of the mishaps, mistakes and misdemeanours along the way and all told in Paul's inimitable style.

Stories include:

- The vicars fallen in the grave!
- Don't worry love; We'll be back for you later
- Tell the priest his handbag's on fire!
- Yes, but his name wasn't Albert!
- Is that a stiff in your hearse or are you just pleased to see me?

Due Summer 2007

IT'S YOUR FUNERAL

by

Paul R Seymour

Other Books by Paul Page

Poems from the Graveyard

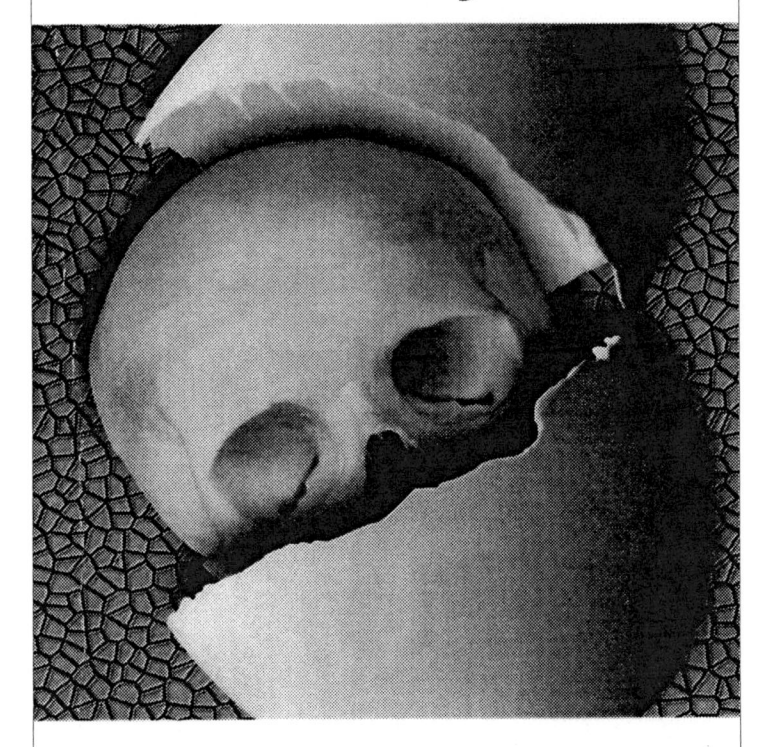

Paul Bearer

If you enjoyed reading this book, why not buy Paul's other books (available from all **BAD** bookstores (or direct from Amazon.co.uk)…

THIS AIN'T Shakespeare
by Paul Bearer

FEATURING:
BBC Award Winning Poem...
GONE FISHING

Poetry for 'normal' people!

Website

You can also see more examples of Paul's work by visiting his website at:

http://members.aol.com/graveyardpoems

Or to order books, leave comments, check for latest updates, publication dates, etc., feel free to email him at graveyardpoems@aol.com

Thanks for taking in interest in my work

Just in case you're wondering what I look like 'now' (2006)

20 Years On...

My *'undertaking days'* are a distant memory now (I left 'the Co-op' in 1982) and a **LOT** has happened since then...

For a few years after I left, I couldn't really make up my mind what I wanted to do with my life/career (I became a milkman, bus driver and 'freezer man' for the local bakery (well, I was used to working around freezers after all!) amongst other things) and lived a period of *relative uncertainty*.

However, having been set up on a 'blind date' with a student midwife just before leaving the profession (she was never short of flowers!) and finding that I had an aptitude for 'IT' I now work **with** my beautiful senior midwife **wife**, (does this mean I have two wives?) **Joanne** on the Delivery Suite of my local hospital where I 'count babies for a living so to speak (and, before you say it; **Yes**, I know! I really have worked at **'both ends of the spectrum'** (or should that now be speculum?) now!

Recently, following the release of two 'relatively acclaimed' poetry books (and various other 'literary and creative projects) I have become a *guest speaker* for the Rotary and Women's Institutes amongst others and now use my 'highly developed' sick sense of humour to try and bring a few smiles to a peoples faces.

I still think back to those 'boyhood days' and can vividly recall many of the incidents written about on the previous pages but, for **now** at least, I'm into *life* **not** death!

Printed in the United Kingdom
by Lightning Source UK Ltd.
132434UK00001B/188/A